no one brings you a casserole

when your husband goes to rehab

LEAH GREY

NO ONE BRINGS YOU A CASSEROLE WHEN YOUR HUSBAND GOES TO REHAB
Copyright © 2021 by Leah Grey

All rights reserved. Neither this publication nor any part of this publication may be reproduced or transmitted in any form or by any means, electronic or mechanical, including photocopying, recording or any information storage and retrieval system, without permission in writing from the author.

The methods described in this book are comprised of personal opinion, testimony, and interpretations of scripture. They are not intended to serve as a definitive set of instructions. The book is not intended to be a substitute for pastoral care or medical advice from a licensed physician.

Scripture quotations have been taken from the Christian Standard Bible®, Copyright © 2017 by Holman Bible Publishers. Used by permission. Christian Standard Bible® and CSB® are federally registered trademarks of Holman Bible Publishers. Scripture marked (NKJV) taken from the New King James Version®. Copyright © 1982 by Thomas Nelson. Used by permission. All rights reserved. Scripture quotations marked (NIV) are taken from the Holy Bible, New International Version®, NIV®. Copyright © 1973, 1978, 1984, 2011 by Biblica, Inc.® Used by permission of Zondervan. All rights reserved worldwide. www.zondervan.com The "NIV" and "New International Version" are trademarks registered in the United States Patent and Trademark Office by Biblica, Inc.® Scripture quotations marked (The Voice) taken from The Voice™. Copyright © 2012 by Ecclesia Bible Society. Used by permission. All rights reserved. Scripture quotations marked (MSG) are taken from THE MESSAGE, copyright © 1993, 2002, 2018 by Eugene H. Peterson. Used by permission of NavPress. All rights reserved. Represented by Tyndale House Publishers, a Division of Tyndale House Ministries. Scripture quotations taken from the Amplified® Bible (AMP), Copyright © 2015 by The Lockman Foundation. Used by permission. www.Lockman.org. Scripture quotations are from the ESV® Bible (The Holy Bible, English Standard Version®), copyright © 2001 by Crossway, a publishing ministry of Good News Publishers. Used by permission. All rights reserved. Scripture quotations marked (ERV) taken from the HOLY BIBLE: EASY-TO-READ VERSION © 2001 by World Bible Translation Center, Inc. and used by permission. Scripture quotations marked (KJV) taken from the Holy Bible, King James Version, which is in the public domain.

Print ISBN: 978-1-4866-2039-5
eBook ISBN: 978-1-4866-2040-1

Word Alive Press
119 De Baets Street, Winnipeg, MB R2J 3R9
www.wordalivepress.ca

Cataloguing in Publication may be obtained through Library and Archives Canada

For Grander, who refused to read past the chapter about the Fish.

Contents

	Acknowledgments	ix
1.	New York	1
2.	The Fish	4
3.	Beckett	7
4.	Glenna	12
5.	Grander	15
6.	Moving	19
7.	Married	23
8.	Denley	26
9.	The Truth	32
10.	Rehab	36
11.	Anxiety	40
12.	Canada	45
13.	One Year	49
14.	Recovery	53
15.	Demons	57
16.	Prophecy	62
17.	Alone	67
18.	Abandoned	71
19.	Angry	78
20.	Growing	85
21.	No	90

22.	Still No	95
23.	I'm Back	101
24.	Relapse	107
25.	Devil Car	113
26.	Blue Eyes	118
27.	Wildflower	121
28.	Oh, Baby	125
29.	Forgiveness	129
30.	Brenda	133
31.	Flora	137
32.	Perfection	142
33.	Skating	148

acknowledgments

I would like to thank the real-life family members, friends, and curly-haired ex-boyfriends portrayed in this book for having had a presence in and impact on my life. I recognize that their memories of the events described in this book will be different than my own, most especially for my husband. They are all kind, honest, good people. This book is not intended to hurt any named or unnamed parties, but to share the raw and honest point of view of a girl who dreamed of romance and a life in New York City.

CHAPTER ONE

new york

For as long as I can remember, I wanted to be a New Yorker.

When I was young, my favourite radio station was a retro one called Froggy94. I was born in 1986, but on my Sony Walkman I sang along to The Shirelles' "Mama Said," The Beach Boys' "Wouldn't It Be Nice," and Frank Sinatra's "New York, New York." When Frank and I sang about being able to make it anywhere if you could make it there, I meant it with every fibre of my being.

I imagined myself strutting down New York's cobblestone streets flaunting a dress much too poufy to wear on a Tuesday, or any day, in my humble, Canadian farm-spattered hometown. It would be my Carrie Bradshaw moment.[1] But I thought it was only a dream and didn't believe God would ever send me to New York, even though I knew deep down it was where I belonged.

In sleepy Port Rowan, Ontario, where everyone knew everyone, my peers listened to the Backstreet Boys and Hansen while I listened to Jann Arden and Celine Dion. I was serious, a deep thinker, and it made me feel different. I never had a lot of friends, although I tried that, too, but the pestilence of high school drama never seemed to escape me.

I figured that if I could just get out of there, if I could just move and leave it all behind, maybe everything would change.

Sure enough, it did.

---

1 Carrie Bradshaw is the lead character of the popular HBO show *Sex and the City*. She works as a newspaper columnist, lives in New York City, and buys fabulous shoes.

In New York, I wasn't loud; I was quiet. I wasn't opinionated; I was average. I wasn't successful, interesting, or really anything special at all; I simply existed, and that was good enough for me. For the first time in my life, I had the freedom to be whoever I wanted, to stop being the girl everyone said I was. Small-town life can write your identity before you even know it yourself, and I was tired of feeling like I didn't belong.

I feel like right now is the time to announce that I need to come out of the closet about something. Ready for it?

I wanted to dress fancy.

Yep. Stupid, isn't it?

I wanted to wear fitted black Calvin Kleins with a white ribbed tank top, rock oversized cat-eye sunglasses in vibrant neon pink, add in a strapping pair of ribbon-tied Manolo Blahniks, grab my Louis Vuitton Multicolore Monogram bag, and have breakfast with a bunch of girlfriends.

Even today, I don't have the girlfriends, the sunnies, or the Manolos, but I do have the bag, the tank, and a pair of black Levis that at least come close to those Calvins. Kinda useless without the breakfast with friends, though, isn't it?

This paradox of almost winning, always being on the sidelines of something wonderful, haunts me everywhere I go. I'm always good, never the best. I study, I plan, I overthink, I work, and I see small fruits of my labour, but it's never enough to survive on. Never enough to feed my family.

When your spouse struggles with addiction and you're not the breadwinner of the family—not to cast a stereotype, but it's a common situation—being financially independent is a big deal. I've often wanted success in my life, but through his addiction I needed it—and needing to be financially successful and wanting to be are not the same thing. One is fuelled by desire, the other by desperation. I was scared all the time. And behind me, chasing me, was the whisper of my past failures: *You can't do it. You're a dumb girl who loves fashion and has no substance. If you were smarter, you wouldn't have dropped out of college. If you were a better daughter, you wouldn't have gotten pregnant at twenty-one. If you were prettier, the Fish wouldn't have spent the night kissing the Beast at the Langton dance in Grade Nine.*

The Fish is the nickname I gave to my childhood crush when I was eleven; he was the one that got away. The girl he dumped me for, I called the Beast. Like, *Beauty and the Beast*. It's mean, I know.

The inside of my brain is a scary place. I used to wonder if everyone spent this much time on the hamster wheel planning their life away. I ran round and round, but I never got anywhere. When you begin to narrate your daily life like a Morgan Freeman documentary, you find yourself counting your lucky stars for evading the looney bin for so many years.

You know what my inner Morgan Freeman said? She said, "I was a 111-pound gingersnap from Mennonite country—fine, 120 pounds after kids—who spent her childhood planning a grand romance and fell in love with New York City. And sometimes, Paris."

My existence was a literal cliché.

As if stereotypicality wasn't enough for me to feel like a loser, everything I ever wanted fell from my grip and shattered. I got closer to my dream than most, which is why it hurt so violently when I lost it.

I couldn't wake up to end my nightmare in the city that never sleeps. I tried praying to God, I tried to fight, and I resolved to become a girlboss, but the wound to my inner child bled through the streets of New York City, one picture at a time.

Smile! There's a fabulous view of Central Park.

Smile! My husband's at The New York Times.

Smile! The pigeon lady is in Washington Square Park. It's like Home Alone *in real life.*

Smile! There's an impromptu concert in the streets. Your husband is there and you aren't.

I couldn't come to terms with what had happened to my dreams. Was it my fault my life had turned out this way? Or were there powers greater than myself hiding in the dark shadows of my carefully curated closet?

New York broke my heart. Not in the way a boyfriend does, though. It was so much more disappointing. I wasn't the wife of addiction; I was the wife of the guy who had it all.

CHAPTER TWO

the fish

I was born in Kitchener-Waterloo, Ontario. The KW, they call it. Why did they combine two cities into one? I have no idea, but I bet there's a story there.

My dad went to school at the University of Waterloo before I was born. Then, in 1988, my family moved from the KW to a little town called Port Rowan. It had a dock with colourful boathouses that extended into Lake Erie, one pharmacy, one grocery store, and one school. There were less than a thousand people who called Port Rowan home, and that included the many farmers, mainly of Mennonite heritage, who lived outside town.

My only sibling was my brother Neil, born in 1989, shortly after we arrived in Port Rowan. My parents, on a faith journey, initially took me and my brother to the local church. As we got a little older, my parents made friends with a few local Mennonite families and the remainder of my childhood was spent in the Mennonite Brethren community.

I thought I was Mennonite, until once at Mennonite family camp one of my parents' friends abruptly told me, "You're not Mennonite!" I suppose I thought it was like being Jewish; you could convert. I loved paska at Easter, I loved my friend's mother's borscht, I loved Mennonite sausage at weddings, but I wasn't Mennonite. I never forgot it after that day.

Port Rowan was a television-worthy place where everyone knew the name of my brother and me, the names of my parents, and even my dog, Tucker. He was a sweet goldendoodle before it became a trendy breed. In fact, we had a neighbour who carried dog treats in his pocket when out walking because he knew he would see my parents with Tucker. I'm not an animal person and didn't like dogs, but Tucker was perfect. I cried for weeks when he went running off to heaven.

You can imagine the culture shock I experienced moving from Mennonite country to New York City. When I was in middle school, it was a totally normal thing to smell manure from the farmer's field nearby. "Ew, they fertilized the field," we'd say at recess.

New York smelled like car exhaust, roasted peanuts, and pee.

I was irritated that I'd grown up sheltered and went as far as to refer to my family as the Brady Bunch. From my young perspective, we were disgustingly perfect. My brother and I looked just liked my parents, and we loved each other, too! It was all so... boring. I didn't appreciate how good I had it because I'd never known anything else.

I wish I had known. Maybe I would have avoided what came later.

Local church girls and I didn't jibe as well as I wanted, with their blond hair, gentle words, and ethical behaviour. How were they so quiet, anyway? I couldn't be that quiet. I tried! I found myself criticizing them internally. Before I knew it, red hair and spitfire opinions flew out of me before they'd been adequately processed and tamed. I was always getting into trouble at youth group, while simultaneously losing the interest of nice, quiet church boys.

This might explain why the first church boy I fell in love with was the one who smoked pot. He was interesting! And so cute, with his blue eyes and curly blond hair. I still like curly hair. Call it a weakness, but send me a boy with a mop of curly hair and I'll be a mud puddle. I just want to touch it. Curly-haired heartbreakers, they are.

I met a few boys who broke my heart, but the blond church boy, later aptly named the Fish, was the biggest heartbreaker of them all. My mother said there were plenty of fish in the sea. But for me, there was only one.

I remember the first day I saw him. He was sitting in church next to the tall, stained-glass windows. The light was shining in, transforming that curly blond hair into a halo. He turned, looked at me, and smiled through long eyelashes. I fell in love right then and there.

I didn't talk to him at first, but I became friends with his sister. Not intentionally, of course. We'd hang out at her house after school and I'd occasionally catch glimpses of her older brother—until one day she brought me a letter to our middle school, written by him.

My heart dropped.

The Fish and I wrote letters back and forth for the next year or so. I treasured those letters. I'm sure his sister wasn't as happy to be the messenger between her brother and her then-best-friend, but she graciously delivered them.

When I got to high school, he and I started dating almost immediately. On our first real date, we went mini-golfing and sat by the lakeshore. We held hands. We kissed. He let me wear his neon green hoodie when it got cold, and he gave me a matching green golf ball to take home. I kept it in the box with his letters.

I was in teenage heaven until one morning, right before the first bell rang for school, a church friend of mine in the Fish's grade told me she had seen him at a dance the night before. That's the night he kissed the Beast.

I burst into tears and cried in the middle of the hallway as I tried to process the news.

I forget what happened the rest of that day. I have a blurry memory of the Beast coming up to me and saying something challenging, while another friend told her to get out of my face. I remember avoiding the Fish until we rode home on the bus and he sat beside me to explain. I don't know what he said; I wasn't listening and it didn't matter.

> That day in ninth grade when I heard that he'd danced with another girl, I allowed Satan to write in my heart the story that I wasn't enough.

From that day forward, my self-worth was measured by how much the Fish cared, called, flip-phone texted, or ICQ'd me. That day in ninth grade when I heard that he'd danced with another girl, I allowed Satan to write in my heart the story that I wasn't enough.

CHAPTER THREE

beckett

I TRIED TO FALL IN LOVE MANY TIMES IN AN EFFORT TO ERASE THE Fish from my mind. Some boys were nice. Others were not. My parents disliked them all. I suppose the ones like Light Bright, a guy who sported neon plugs in his ears, didn't look like Brady Bunch material, but he was among my favourites.

In my small-town bedroom, *Vogue* magazine cutouts plastering the lavender-coloured walls, I pined over the Fish until I was seventeen and went off to university.

Finally, independence! I thought. *I can use that fake ID I found on the sidewalk.*

I was going to be a writer. Or a singer. Or a psychologist. Or work in advertising. I would absolutely find the new love of my life. Whatever career I eventually settled on, I believed I would be a total success.

Then I failed my business class.

My class attendance, or lack thereof, became a joke among my dormmates, who started keeping a tally on the wall. That first semester, twenty-four classes attended. Mostly Bs. Not bad. Second semester, twelve classes. Bs, a C, and then the business class. I think I went to business class once, because it took place very early in the morning. It's ironic, as I now love business. But I still hate mornings.

Talk about the enemy messing with your future! He does that, you know. Satan messes with our destiny, finding ways to deter us from every path of success.

The business class probably would have launched me into superwoman territory, navigating the cobblestone streets of New York's West Village in Manolos. The enemy certainly didn't want that.

Growing up in a small town made getting away with shenanigans difficult, so it wasn't until university that I really let loose. At least, I thought I did. Compared to what I later learned in New York, I was a sheltered saint. My small-town rebellions were nothing more than child's play.

While in university, I pursued my love for music. I sang choruses and background music in bars for a rap crew. Didn't see that one coming, did you? I was dating one of them, and looking back now it's one of the most fun times in my life. My parents thought I'd gone off the deep end, I'm sure, but I wasn't getting into as much trouble as you'd think. We drank a lot of tea, occasionally smoked pot, had a drink or two, watched movies, and wrote music.

I made good friends during that period of my life. The musicians understood me. For the first time, I connected with people who thought the same way I did. Deep thinkers, big feelers. And it was nice to find a place where I belonged.

I wish I could tell you that was the end of the Fish, that I picked up my broken heart, took a lesson in self-worth, and never dated him again. But it's not true. The truth is that I dated him again, and again. Many more times... that year, the next year, until my nineteenth birthday when he didn't come to my birthday party and I found out the next day he had gone out with another girl.

How many times would I let him break my heart in the same way? Even though we stopped dating, he remained in the back of my mind.

Over the next few months, a lot happened. The Fish got another girl pregnant, and you can imagine how much that one broke my heart. I got very depressed and lost myself for a while. Suddenly, nothing mattered. There were parties, drinking, and drugs. I felt as though my life was already ruined. I even dropped out of college.

Shortly after, I got pregnant.

Another girl from church had gotten pregnant the year before me, and she'd gone up to the front of the church to make a public apology for her behaviour. After seeing what happened to her, I decided the only thing to do was marry my baby's father. It was the only way to right the wrong and avoid public humiliation. So I married my son's father in an attempt to atone for my sins, but it was a mistake.

My pregnancy was difficult. I had pains when I stood for long periods of time and ended up being flown to the hospital twice in a helicopter. On one of those hospitalizations, the paramedic performed and danced a Michael Jackson song down the hall to calm me down. God bless the paramedics!

The second time, the hospital kept me on bedrest. I spent four months there, many miles away from friends and family. I was allowed five-minute showers and spent the rest of the time confined to my bed. It wasn't what I had pictured doing at twenty-one, that's for certain.

The doctors kept telling me my son might die. I was experiencing cervical funnelling and had a high risk of preterm labour. But I didn't believe them and grew very protective of his life. At twenty-four weeks gestation, the nurses pushed me in a wheelchair through the neonatal unit and showed me what my baby would look like if he was born at one pound, then three pounds, then five. They gave me a handful of neonatal diapers, in increasing sizes, to hang on to. As each week passed, I smugly threw the smaller of them in the trash.

Being in the hospital was tough, especially because I'd smoked occasionally until the day I was admitted. But I wasn't in love with my son's father and the hospital was a welcome escape from the marriage I'd never wanted.

By thirty-two weeks, I was tired of being in the hospital and being on lockdown and begged to return home. The hospital relented.

But within days I was back in my obstetrician's office with more pain. The obstetrician scheduled an induction around thirty-six weeks and my family came over for the weekend. It was Thanksgiving and we ate turkey and went to a park. The next morning, I gave birth to my son Beckett, who was a whopping preterm eight pounds, two ounces.

Life as a young mother was hard, and I was extremely critical of myself for the drastic turn my life had taken. Instead of graduating with my degree and starting a new successful career, I was changing diapers and cleaning up spittle. I felt stuck in my marriage and was the only one in my group of friends who had a child. I loved my son, but I didn't love the choices I'd made at such a young age.

On December 21, 2008, when my son was three months old, all three of us were driving home for Christmas just outside Ajax, Ontario. My cat, Stella, was in the car, too. It was cold and the roads were slick with ice. I watched as the SUV in front of us came to a sudden stop. We hit the brakes, but our car slid. I stretched my arms out in front of me to brace myself for the crash as we slammed into the SUV. The hood of our vehicle flew up into the air—and stopped right before it crushed us. Angels, no doubt.

Our airbags never deployed.

My son screamed in the back of the car. I shakily picked up my phone and dialled the only number I could think to call: my mother.

"Mom? I'm okay, don't worry," I said. "We got into an accident and we hit the car in front of us."

My mother's sister, Cindy, had died in a car accident when she was sixteen. My parents had told me to make sure if I was ever in an accident, I always started my phone call with whether or not I was okay.

She shouted for my dad, then asked me where we were.

"I don't know," I replied. "Somewhere outside of Toronto."

"We're on our way," Dad said. "We'll call when we get to Toronto and you can let us know where you are."

The drive from Ajax to Port Rowan is more than two hundred kilometres and it takes about three hours. I feel like my parents got there within the hour, but that's probably because my mind was a blur.

When the paramedics arrived, I was scared to pick up my son and they told me to leave him in his car seat until the doctor had a chance to look at him. He cried for hours, all the way to the hospital, and he kept crying while we waited for the doctor. Finally, he was cleared as being perfectly fine.

Now that I'm the mother of three, I wish I had ignored the paramedics and picked him up. The sweet thing was scared.

I suffered many injuries from that crash, and they got worse as time went on. I ended up having to move home so my parents could help take care of my son. I suffered terrible whiplash and couldn't bend over. My jaw would lock, my arms hurt excruciatingly, I had headaches, I was often dizzy, my hips had been thrown out of alignment, and my sciatica had been pinched. It took seven years for my body to heal.

The worst part was the post-traumatic stress. Every time I saw headlights, I had flashbacks of that accident. It left me scared to drive. And my poor baby boy woke up in the night many times with a jolt, crying. We were both traumatized by the experience.

Oh, and my cat? Stella was also fine. She had been in her cat carrier and remained the same miserable grump she'd always been.

CHAPTER FOUR

glenna

In January 2010, I applied for a legal separation from my son's father.

Of all the ways I had failed in life, being a divorced Christian carried the most shame. After all, the Bible talked about forgiveness for sexual sin, but not divorce.

Due to my increasing distress and shame, my mom recommended I visit her friend, Glenna Pearl. I was sceptical, to say the least. Go talk to an old lady? Why?

But the moment I sat down with Glenna, I knew there was a reason I had walked through her door. Without me having said a word, she knew things I wasn't wise enough to see myself. Seniors are the pearls of the world.

Glenna was a widow, her husband Arthur having gone to heaven a few years prior. She happily shared her memories of him as her dangling earrings twinkled.

One of the first pearls of wisdom Glenna gave me had to do with the word *annulment*. When she asked about my marriage, I told her everything that had transpired in my life up until that point: the Fish, my broken heart, leaving college, the parties, my pregnancy, and my shame over wanting a divorce. Glenna then assured me that God had annulled my marriage.

Suddenly, all the guilt I'd been carrying around exploded into a worn pillow on her flowery green couch that smelled like grace.

I wanted to believe what Glenna said, but I had no frame of reference to believe it. I hadn't before met anyone who heard God like that, and I wondered if she might be psychic—or worse, senile.

I submitted the divorce papers to our local courthouse after two years of separation, and much to my surprise they responded that they couldn't grant our divorce because there was no record of our marriage.

I did some digging and discovered that the paperwork from the pastor who had married us had never been filed with the government, even though he had mailed it in.

It was all the confirmation I needed: God had miraculously annulled my marriage.

For the purposes of custody, my child's father and I needed to file for both the marriage and the divorce on the same day. Even though I struggled with a lot of shame over my first marriage, I don't regret having my son or trying to do what was best for him. Beckett was the most incredible boy. I wish I could go back to the beginning and love him all over again. God used his life to pull me out of a pit of despair, and it was through his birth that I learned God speaks to us.

My time with Glenna was precious as I grew in my faith and learned how to have a more intimate relationship with God. In 2011, I had the honour of helping Glenna put her life's story into a book for her family. She'd survived spinal meningitis without antibiotics in the 1940s and bought her first fur coat from her teacher's salary in 1954, to wear on a trip to New York to visit her aunt Olive. She and I had a lot in common.

She had a simple approach to faith and believed that accepting God's love for us was all we needed to do in order to feel fulfilled. She once said, "Imagination is more important than knowledge." That became a lifelong source of inspiration to me.

Glenna even tried to help me forget the Fish, but it didn't work. I prayed for God to take the love away. I tried to hate him, but I couldn't. When none of that worked, I wrote songs, sung my heart out, and dreamt of moving away.

Every year, our town had an art festival. Everyone would come. In a small town, everyone comes to everything.

I attended the festival with my son, daydreaming as usual, and walking backward because… I don't know. But as usually happens when one walks backward, I bumped into someone. Whoops!

I spun around and found myself two inches away from a stranger's face. Well, that would have been awkward enough, but this was no stranger. It was him.

"Oh… it's you," I eloquently said.

The Fish smiled, put his hand on my arm, and said, "Look out."

In perfect romance movie timing, I dropped my purse.

Bending down to pick my dignity off the pavement, I noticed that he was holding some girl's hand while I played out the rom-com in my head. I collected my thoughts and decided I was over him. Then I said goodbye to the Fish for the very last time.

Many years later, I was asked by a well-respected Christian pastor and author what I loved about the Fish. The best answer I could come up with was "I don't know. I liked his eyes." I felt embarrassed. After years of chasing after him, I couldn't even say what I loved about him.

The pastor laughed a bit. "You know, it's true what they say about the eyes being the windows to the soul. When someone says they loved someone's eyes, it usually means they fell in love with their soul."

The second he said it, I knew it was true. It wasn't the Fish's bright green hoodie, his crooked smile, or his funny artwork I had loved; it was just him. I felt like my soul had been married to his from the start.

For many years after, I looked for that same kind of soul connection. Until one cold, snowy New Year's Eve in 2012.

CHAPTER FIVE

grander

"What are you doing tonight?" asked my co-worker at the hair salon.

"Nothing," I replied.

"Why?"

"I never do anything for New Year's Eve."

But inside I was thinking, *Because I have a kid, you dummy*. New Year's Eve isn't a night for single mothers. It's for couples who want to kiss at midnight and single people who are looking for lovers. I was neither of those things.

"Come out with us," she said.

"Where are you going?"

"Niagara Falls. We're going to a concert. You're young… you should come! It'll be fun!"

Before I knew what was happening, two more of my co-workers joined in. So I called my parents and asked if they would watch Beckett, who had just turned four years old. With obvious disapproval, they begrudgingly agreed.

At the time, I was working two jobs and living in a townhouse. I'd gotten my hairstyling license a few years prior so I would have a job to support my son, and now I was working full-time at a hair salon called The Gay Blade. Interesting name, but it doesn't mean what you think; the owner's name was Gay.

My other job was at the only fashion-forward dress shop in our area. I closed up at the salon and quickly drove to the dress shop to find an outfit. I bought a black-sequined wrap dress and paired it with combat boots and a gorgeous black and grey polished stone necklace. Perfect.

I brought no alcohol with me that night. We got to our hotel in Niagara Falls, then headed to the concert. The performer was a dubstep artist called DeadMau5. It wasn't anything I normally listened to, but it was fun. The girls from work were joined by a bigger group of their friends and we drifted away from one another as the night went on.

A few of my brother's friends were there, too, so I spent most of the evening hanging out with them. They felt more like family.

As the concert drew to a close, I went to the coat check to retrieve my jacket. I had shared a hanger with the girls from work to save money, and one of them had accidentally taken my coat with them. I stood there for a while, trying to figure out what I would do next. The temperature outside was well below freezing and I didn't look forward to walking in the cold to our hotel in my wrap dress. Wind and wrap dresses don't go well together.

One of my brother's friends lent me his jacket and said he would pick it up from me in the morning. Grateful, I went outside to look for the girls from the salon.

Being a small girl, I was always nervous going out at night by myself. I stood under the streetlight in case any midnight perverts tried to attack me. Surely if they did, someone would see me screaming under the light instead of hidden away in the shadows.

Suddenly, I heard someone yell, "What are you doing there?"

"Who, me?" I asked, looking around.

"Yes, you. Why are you all alone?" The faceless male voice was coming from a crowd of people across the road.

"I can't find my friends."

"Come over here. We'll help you find them," the voice called.

"No, thanks. I don't know you."

"Okay. Well, we'll just wait here until you find them and make sure you're okay."

By this point, I could see that the guy was part of a group of men and women. Although I stayed on my side of the street, I thought it was nice of them to wait with me. As promised, the strangers stood there, waiting to see if I successfully spotted my co-workers.

Eventually I decided they were safe and crossed the road.

"Hi," I said.

"Hello," the guy said. "I'm Grander."

Grander asked me where I was from and I told him about how I'd lost my coat and friends. He introduced his friends to me, Mark and J.J. There were more of them in the group, but the others slowly dispersed to find food and I was left with the three guys.

Grander offered to walk me back to my hotel. He was extremely friendly and told me he was visiting Canada from New York.

New York? I thought. *Interesting.*

On our walk, he showed me photos of his son and friended me on Facebook. When we got close to the hotel, I said goodbye and ran inside. After all, I didn't want to get myself into a compromising situation alone with three strange men!

We took a photo before I ran off, though. I didn't know at the time this would be the first photo I'd take with my husband. Had I known, I wouldn't have stood there in my brother's friend's big ugly coat.

> He was extremely friendly and told me he was visiting Canada from New York. *New York?* I thought. *Interesting.*

Grander texted me all night and into the next morning. I looked him up on Facebook the next day and was surprised at how good-looking he was. I was even more surprised that I hadn't noticed this the night before! And New York… it had to be fate.

From then on, we never stopped talking. Our chats lasted far into the early morning hours and it's a wonder either of us was able to get any work done at all. I guess people have a lot more stamina when they're young and in love.

We had our first date in February 2013, with Grander catching the last plane to Toronto during a blizzard while I caught the last train to the city. After that, we saw one another almost every other weekend. Grander usually was the one to drive nine hours to see me, and eventually I took my first plane ride to visit him in New York. Shortly after, we went on a five-day trip to the Dominican Republic, where he'd grown up.

By April, he had proposed.

By June, I told my family I was moving to New York. They weren't pleased.

"You're making a mistake," my dad said.

"What do you even know about this guy?" asked my mom.

I felt indignant. I told my parents about all our midnight talks and assured them that I *did* know him. I was in love and I was going.

I was the same lover of curly-headed guys I'd always been, and I fell hard for Grander. There was something about him that felt both wild and comfortable. He looked at me in much the same way the Fish had, through long eyelashes and carefully reserved smiles.

I suppose that's why they call it "being swept off your feet." I was knocked over, and enjoying the fall.

He was the one I'd been looking for. His zest for life and adventurous attitude made my own wild spirit soar. We would live in New York and have the most perfect mixed race babies with the most beautiful eyelashes and dark eyebrows. It had to be fate.

Finally, I put to rest sixteen years of hoping the Fish would somehow find his way back to me. What I didn't know was that my heart would hit the floor many times down the road.

CHAPTER SIX

moving

MOVING TO NEW YORK WAS EVERYTHING I'D EVER DREAMED OF. Before moving, I had already planned all the details of our apartment overlooking the city. It would be small, but it'd be all right. Mid-century modern with a hint of Scandinavia and plenty of white. Modern and classy.

I should have known New York would let me down when my son and I moved into what was supposed to be a temporary, bachelor-sized apartment in Jersey City Heights. Nothing against New Jersey, of course. My opinion, previously formed by what I'd seen on television—hello, *Jersey Shore*—improved significantly after living there. The community was more family-oriented than anything I found in Manhattan.

Those born and bred in Jersey are loud, unashamed, and love their mamas. Exactly like my boys. And with the exception of the accent, the inner parts of New Jersey felt just like Canada. It was like being home, but with more sports and coffee (pronounced *caw-fee*).

I later tried to eat Italian food in Canada, but fuhgeddaboudit. New Jersey has the best Italian food, bar none. You can buy freshly made soft mozzarella every day in the grocery store. Canadian mozzarella is hard and tastes waxy.

Despite the positives, I was still let down upon my arrival. You might think it was the five flights of stairs I had to climb juggling groceries and a child. Possibly, it was the lack of sleep due to constant noise from police and ambulance sirens, neighbourhood dogs, and late-night party people. A girl from the country wasn't used to any of that.

It could have been the surprising prejudice I felt living in a Hispanic neighbourhood. Turns out gringa is not a compliment, by the way.

One day, I took my laundry to the wash-and-fold Grander went to. I was excited to have someone wash and fold all my laundry for only fifteen dollars. But they sent me away with a run of Spanish sentences, fingers wagging all the while. I hoped I was imagining it, but I didn't think they wanted to do my laundry; they did it for Grander.

I would have done the laundry myself except that the complex had the smallest coin laundry machines I had ever seen. The laundry room was in a dingy basement down another two flights of stairs from the main entry. In total there were seven flights of stairs, three loads of toddler laundry, plus three dollars to wash and dry every load. This meant I was spending nine dollars to climb forty-two flights of stairs.

It was worth the extra six dollars to go to the wash-and-fold, even with the occasional piece of a stranger's clothing that came home with ours. I most commonly found other people's socks, but once I found a pair of pink underwear.

Maybe the communal washer in our apartment building isn't such a bad idea, I thought. *After all, how would I ever know if Grander was staying faithful?*

We moved fifteen days later.

Happy isn't a strong enough word to describe what moving into our new apartment felt like. At $1,350 per month, the price was right, and it was reasonably new-looking. Unfortunately, we were in the same neighbourhood. But it was a much bigger apartment, if six hundred fifty square feet can be considered "big" for a family of three. We had two bedrooms, a patio, and even a small backyard.

The apartment sat kiddy-corner to a park that boasted a farmer's market every Saturday, and it was right around the corner from the coolest coffee shop in Jersey City Heights. It didn't matter to us that the apartment's lack of interior windows made it look more like a bowling alley than a home. To me, it was perfect.

The best part? We were on the first floor, and there was a clean laundromat on the corner. I only had to drag my laundry thirty feet. Excellent upgrade.

Of all the places I've lived, and there have been quite a few, that apartment turned out to be my least favourite. It was the first place where New York would break my heart.

New York is said to be the city of dreams, but those who coined that phrase left out the fact that the air is thick with disappointment, poverty, and struggle. New Yorkers are tough because they have to be to survive. It is a dysfunctional family living in close quarters and barely speaking to each other. That said, when push comes to shove and disaster strikes, New Yorkers always stick together; they don't abandon family.

And yet the most beautiful thing about New York is that its hard streets can lead you to find what you're really made of. If you work hard enough, you can be any version of yourself you'd like to be. There's no guarantee you'll be a success, but it doesn't matter because you come out of it changed. It is the love story of New York.

I experienced intense culture shock from moving to the city. Everything was new and chaotic. In the town I'd grown up in, the closest bus station had been an hour away.

Forever the optimist, I was determined to figure out the survival skills I would need in order to make it in one of the world's most iconic urban jungles.

For example, if you want to turn left, when the traffic light turns green you are to go fast, before the oncoming cars begin driving through. Sure, you run the risk of being hit and dying in a car crash. But you'll probably make it. It's like a game of chicken, and you can't be the loser. Even though it isn't legal, everyone expects you to drive like a maniac.

Another lesson was to stare straight ahead when walking down the street and not look anyone in the eye. If no one asks you to go on a bus tour, it means you're passing as a New Yorker. You absolutely don't want to look like a dreaded tourist.

If you pass someone who looks intimidating, make direct eye contact and telepathically communicate, *I'll rip your face off if you touch me.* They'll silently get the message that you mean business and turn their attention elsewhere.

Alternatively, they may take note that you're not a tourist and give you a nod of approval.

Helicopter parenting in New York is okay. In fact, it's expected. The parks aren't safe and no one is to be trusted. Ever. Don't let your child out of your sight or you could be on the news that night. You don't want to be on the news.

Like a hidden gem, the view of the city skyline from New Jersey is an iconic picture. So many people visit New York and never bother to see it from the other side of the Hudson River. You don't want to miss that view.

We lived directly across the Hudson from Chelsea Piers and would hang out on the rooftop of our building, enjoying the Manhattan skyline. It was truly breathtaking. I have an image seared into my memory of a harvest moon rising over the city. In those moments, New York was the love story I had imagined it to be and more.

With my rose-coloured perspective, the happiest chapter of my life turned into the kind of nightmare I could have never imagined. And yet, through everything we went through together, New York left me stronger. Which is good, because I don't know that I could have managed the heartbreak otherwise.

CHAPTER SEVEN

married

Life was good. Really good.

We were living in our bowling alley apartment and my days were filled with warm weather, farmer's markets, and hipster coffees.

My son and I loved to explore New York while Grander was at work. We rode in with him in the morning and would spend the rest of the day wandering the city or lounging in Central Park. We'd take a ferry to the Statue of Liberty, see the Brooklyn Flea Market, or explore the Lincoln Center before meeting my husband for lunch wherever he was in the city that day.

We were still engaged but planning for our wedding, which was to take place in the Dominican Republic. But in a moment of spontaneity, we decided to elope that summer. We planned to have a small ceremony in New York, then hold a real wedding the following spring in the Dominican with our friends and family. I didn't like "living in sin" prior to marriage, so this idea soothed my conscience.

I planned to wear the asymmetrical black dress I had brought with me from Canada and purchase a pair of sparkly pink retro-style high heels. That week, Beckett went to visit my parents and his birth father in Canada, leaving Grander and me alone. We set a date with the courthouse in New York to be married on August 2nd.

When the day of our impromptu wedding arrived, Grander had to work for part of the morning. I was nervous heading into the city alone, since I wasn't yet used to public transportation, so I drove in with him, bringing my dress and my shoes.

I spent the morning alone. Unsure what to do with myself, I wandered around Times Square and went up a side street. I found a fancy breakfast place and got a table for one.

Sitting alone in a restaurant the morning of your wedding in a city of eight million people is a lonely, harrowing feeling. My inner Morgan Freeman kept asking, *Do you really think you belong here?*

I ordered coffee with cream (I took cream back then), ate a croissant with strawberry jam, and imagined I was a mysterious French girl.

I called my mom with a smile on my face, but it broke my heart. I wanted my family with me. What was I doing? Why wasn't my son with me? I wished I could push pause on our plans, but my desire to get married was greater than my desire to stop it.

I waited in the cafe until Grander was done work, sometime around eleven in the morning. Wandering around the city alone was far too sad and I'd already put on my wedding makeup. I didn't want to muck it up by crying.

Grander took me to his friend's hair salon and she did a classic low updo for me. I put on the black and pink sunglasses I'd bought at the grocery store, and together we went to the courthouse.

We met two of Grander's friends there, Mark from New Year's Eve and a guy named Jason. We signed the paperwork and waited with a multitude of same-sex couples. Gay marriage had been legalized in New York in 2011, but the rush of nuptials peaked in 2013. One of the grooms told me I looked fabulous; it perked me up a bit.

The ceremony was very basic. I've been to courthouse weddings since then and ours was as simple as it gets.

"Do you want traditional vows, civil vows, or did you bring your own?" the officiant asked.

"Traditional?" I said hesitantly.

Grander and I looked at one another, not entirely sure what traditional meant.

She then asked us to repeat after her: "To have and to hold, from this day forward, for better, for worse, for richer, for poorer, in sickness and in health…"

Then she pronounced us married. We kissed briefly and then it was over. It took no more than five minutes.

We left the courthouse to celebrate with champagne and my husband's friends. We had drinks on the rooftops of Koreatown and danced in a lounge on the Lower East Side. And then we went home.

Your wedding is supposed to be the happiest day of your life, but I felt very alone. I was glad to marry Grander, but I had none of my people there. I wanted to share that day with my parents, brother, and friends. I told myself I would feel better after we'd had our Dominican wedding and that this was just the legal portion.

I didn't know that the day I was looking forward to would never come.

CHAPTER EIGHT

denley

A FEW MONTHS AFTER GETTING MARRIED, I BECAME PREGNANT AGAIN. And three days after we joyously celebrated the pregnancy, Grander went missing.

I kept calling his phone, but he didn't answer. I spent the rest of the night hyperventilating on the bathroom floor, clutching my stomach and stifling sobs so I didn't wake my son. I prayed for my panic to stop, but it didn't. I eventually passed out in bed from exhaustion.

Sometime in the early morning, Grander finally answered the phone. He told me he had stopped at Mark's house on his way home from work and there had been a party. He'd slept there.

Hours after his call, he dragged himself through the front door and passed out on my son's bunkbed. He looked horrible, and I reeled with anger. I dumped a bowl of water on his head and he sat up in shock before immediately passing out again.

Not a word. Up and out.

Promptly, I left with Beckett, telling him we were going on an adventure. We drove to a nearby hotel in the middle of a blizzard. Well, a New Jersey blizzard isn't much more than an average day of snowfall in Canada. It was nothing out of the ordinary for us.

When I was a single mother, I loved taking my son to hotels for an adventure. It was fun to play in the pool and eat continental breakfast. Also, it was the only kind of vacation I could afford.

Late that night, my husband finally awoke from his stupor and saw that we were gone. He became increasingly worried that his newly pregnant wife was out in a "blizzard." Meanwhile, my son and I somersaulted back and forth on hotel beds, dreaming we were Olympians. I didn't answer Grander's persistent phone calls or tell anyone where we were, in fear that they might let him know we were okay. I wanted him to feel my pain. I wanted him to believe that we were dead and it was his fault. I wanted him to be wracked with guilt and condemnation.

I was too naive to know it at the time, but all I did was pettily inflict great pain on someone I loved. I had been right to go to a hotel, but wrong to try and hurt him.

I returned home and we worked it out. Grander was sorry for the way he'd acted and we carried on being happy.

Something had changed for me that day, though. It was our first fight. My knight-in-shining armour, my James Bond tech genius, my sexy New Yorker husband, had hurt me. I had thought myself a good judge of character, but I was suddenly filled with doubt—not only about my ability to judge a person's character, but about everything in my life. Had my parents been right? Had it been a mistake to move to New York and marry Grander?

Over the course of the following year, I noticed that he drank more than normal. He didn't get drunk, but it was more than what I thought the average person should drink for a healthy lifestyle.

"Why are you drinking whiskey again?" I'd ask. "It's the middle of the week."

"It's just a little bit."

But it was a little bit, a lot of the time.

"Grander, you already had two," I'd point out after dinner.

"Just a little bit more." And he would have another glass.

I had no previous experience with addiction. No one in my immediate circle had been an alcoholic or drug addict. None of my friends had been to rehab. Most of the people I'd grown up with had been Mennonites who didn't drink, or barely drank. It had been noteworthy when one of my friend's parents had a beer, scandalous when they would smoke a cigar! My parents had always had a healthy relationship with alcohol and I'd never noticed them have more than two glasses of anything.

So when Grander started drinking more, I took him at his word: it was just a little bit.

I found myself regretting our speedy romance and wishing I had taken more time to get to know the man I'd married. Maybe if we had dated longer, I would have paid more attention to the warning signs.

Then again, maybe not. Some people are so good at hiding their secrets that you'll never see those secrets—until they become impossible to ignore. No one plans for their lives to turn into an episode of *Intervention*.

I told Grander that I was concerned about his drinking and he agreed to talk to his friend, who was an addiction counsellor. He started going to Alcoholics Anonymous with that friend every week. He completely stopped drinking and I once again felt sure he was the superhero I had always thought he was.

> Some people are so good at hiding their secrets that you'll never see those secrets—until they become impossible to ignore.

My dreams of being self-sufficient were fading fast, but I kept my hopes up and waited for my American work permit to arrive. By the time I received it, I was very pregnant.

During all this, I was also managing a high-risk pregnancy because of my previous experience with Beckett. It was an irritable, can't-do-anything kind of pregnancy. I put myself on bedrest, as per the advice of my rockstar doctor, David Principe. He was a total godsend.

Dr. P was a classic, good-looking New Jersey Italian. He was direct and didn't tolerate baloney—and that's the nicest way to say it!—but he had a heart the size of the tristate area. He emotionally sustained me through my husband's emerging addiction and was a great source of support. Without his guidance, I'm certain my fears would have destroyed me.

God had clearly spoken, so I set aside my dreams of working once more. I was the everyday housewife, right? I could feel my inner Melanie

Griffith[2] fading away until the gaps on my resume read "Can successfully wash two loads of laundry per day, cleans up nappies one-handed with effortless efficiency, excellent at driving children to and from extracurricular whilst simultaneously serving dinner on time."

Christmas came and went that year. My husband was sober and we took a trip south to Myrtle Beach with my parents and made memories I still smile back on.

After we got back from the trip, we moved to a bigger apartment in Union City in anticipation of the baby. It was my favourite of all the places we lived. At $2,650 per month, plus another $150 for parking, it was twice the cost and size of our last apartment. And it was brand-new. It had three bedrooms, two bathrooms, plenty of windows, and in-suite laundry. No more laundromats, praise the good Lord!

As an added bonus, we had a view of Manhattan from the living room window.

A large bakery resided on the corner of our street, and our parking lot always smelled like cinnamon buns. For a pregnant girl in the city, it was sweet reverie. Fresh Portuguese rolls, New York bagels, Jersey donuts, and authentic empanadas tempted me, their savoury smells drifting through our open windows.

Union City was vibrant and interesting. A nearby couple danced Merengue on their rooftop, teenagers snuck out for cigarettes across the road, and much to my heart's delight, a neighbour across the way played the saxophone. I'd listen to him play the sounds of New York while remembering when my neighbour across the street in Port Rowan, Ontario had learned to play the drums. It was a time of reflection on how far I had come.

The new apartment brought new hope. I was glad to be out of the bowling alley apartment, but I found domestic life stressful. Between Grander and me, we had two boys with another child on the way, and I still felt disappointment over having to push pause on my hairstyling career. I'd always wanted to be like the savvy businesswomen in the movies,

---

2   Melanie Griffith plays Tess in *Working Girl*, an ambitious stockbroker's secretary who pretends to be her boss after her boss steals her idea and pitches it to a client.

but I related more to the sad woman secretly smoking away her troubles out a bathroom window.

Had I been created to be this weary, defeated, helpless version of myself? No. She was the version of myself Satan had convinced me I was. Instead of believing in the role God had for my life, I made that tired and weary soul the heroine of my story. She was weird, and weird was cool. She was moody, and moody was mysterious. She was spontaneous, and curly-haired boys love a girl who's spontaneous. She wasn't a nice, quiet, blond church girl who never said anything out of line; she was wild and free.

With everything I'd ever dreamed about calling to me through my living room window, I should have felt the most free I'd ever felt. Instead I was paralyzed. I worried Grander might pick up drinking again, because that's what the Al-Anon[3] literature told me would happen. I hadn't made many friends and felt lonely with all the hours Grander spent working. When had I signed up to become a stay-at-home mom of three?

I decided to watch every season of *Pretty Little Liars* and forget my troubles.[4] Girl meets boy. Boy kisses girl. Girl falls in love. Boy kisses a new girl. The first girl is brokenhearted, and so on.

Like the romance playing out on my screen, if we could just see our relationships through God's eyes, we would know what was coming when it wasn't going to go well. But it's much harder to have an objective point of view when you're the main character.

God does give us warnings, but more often He gives us the gift of learning important lessons. Painful experiences help us to become more mature. If we knew ahead of time everything that would hurt us, we would avoid the pain and never change. A life without risk is one without growth.

God has the perfect perspective of our lives, which is why we must always keep His will in our line of vision. If we had His point of view, we would see that there was a grander story being written. No pun intended!

In July 2014, one month before my due date, I went into the hospital in the middle of the night with labour pains. Dr. P burst in wearing a

---

3   A support group for family members and friends of alcoholics.
4   The characters of Ezra and Caleb were particularly helpful.

leather jacket and boots to match, his motorcycle helmet tucked under his arm.

"Let's do this, rockstar," he said, calm as could be.

In less than thirty minutes I gave birth to my second son, Denley, who weighed a mere five pounds, eleven ounces. Grander showed up at the hospital looking gaunt, like he'd been the one to give birth. I knew something was wrong.

My husband went back to work that night in the city and I spent the remainder of my time in the hospital alone, wondering if he would tell me his secrets.

CHAPTER NINE

the truth

I WOKE UP AND THE SUN WAS SHINING ON ANOTHER BEAUTIFUL DAY. The pitter-patter of little feet echoed through the apartment as I stretched to roll over in bed.

One more moment of peace and I'll get up.

"Mom! Wake up!" Beckett said while standing on the chest at the end of the bed before launching his small body into the air and landing on me full-force.

"Wahhh!"

And there's the baby, I thought. *Time to start another day!*

We ate breakfast and I got the children ready for a day of play. Grander had left for work hours before, not eating breakfast before he left. Nothing new there.

I wondered if I should try to squeeze in a short Bible study, but it was getting late in the day already and I decided to do it later. Instead I turned on some worship music and began to tidy the house. One of the benefits of apartment living is how easy it is to clean. For a semi-compulsive tidier, it helped my state of mind to maintain a clean home.

I packed our stroller and knocked on my neighbour Alicia's door to see if she wanted to go to the park with me.

When we'd moved into the neighbourhood, my mom, who unlike me is very friendly by nature, introduced us as a way to help me make a friend. Alicia and I were both hairstylists, both pregnant at the time, and we lived one floor away from one another. She'd had her son one month before me, and her friendship was a godsend. She was outgoing, friendly, and had an acute interest in healthy food, as did I. She and her husband, who was a chef by trade, were very good cooks.

Alicia and I walked with the children to the expansive park up the road. We caught a few rays of sun while rocking the babies in their strollers, watching as Beckett showed us how well he could climb now that he was five. The birds were singing and our dynamic neighbourhood was filled with parents conversing in different dialects; it's beautiful how laughter sounds the same in every language.

Suddenly, I felt like cooking.

Alicia and I returned to our apartment building, we said goodbye, and a few groceries later our home was filled with the smell of a simple homemade *coq au vin*. It was a favourite family recipe inherited from someone's grandmother (not mine). I preferred to cook meals slow and long, which gave me an opportunity to do the Bible study I'd skipped that morning. The baby napped and Beckett watched a show, so I thought I'd better take advantage of the quiet.

Feeling totally *hygge*,[5] I settled into a spot of sunlight by the window and opened my Bible.

"Wahhh!"

Not again, I thought, feeling frustrated. *Okay, I'll deal with the baby and then find some quiet time.*

One hour and five Lego houses later, I finally returned to my quiet space—just as the oven timer began beeping at me. It was time to make my side dishes and finish dinner. My Bible study would have to wait.

With the prep done and dinner ready, it was nearing six-thirty. Grander was late, as usual. He'd probably eaten at work again.

Asserting my boundaries, I served family dinner without him. It was delicious. Fragrant and comforting.

I left the dishes so I could bathe the children. Jammies on. Stories read. Prayers sent to heaven.

---

5   A Danish word for an atmosphere of coziness, often experienced with family, friends, homemade food, and candles.

Shortly after turning out the lights, I heard the front door open. Finally, there he was.

"Hello," I said.

Grander wouldn't look me in the eye. "Hi."

"How was your day?"

"Long," he replied, signalling that he was tired and didn't want to talk.

"Your dinner is in the fridge."

"Thanks."

He took a minuscule amount of food and sat down at the table. I sat down, too. He looked haggard and perturbed at my presence.

"Why were you so late?" I asked.

"I was working."

"Working on what?" I knew I was walking on dangerous ground now.

"Just working."

He made eye contact for the first time and tried to keep his face straight to prove he wasn't lying. But I could see something was wrong in his eyes. It's about that time that I started to suspect he wasn't drinking, but doing drugs.

"Okay," I said.

At one point, I would have stayed there and pressed him about why he'd gotten home so late, which would have led to an argument. Since the baby had been born, Grander was distancing himself from me more and more. He always said he was working, and maybe he was, but he never shared details of his day with me. I remembered how my parents used to talk about their day at the dinner table and missed my Brady Bunch life.

I felt as suspicious as I did rejected.

Where was he? I wondered as I retreated to our bedroom. *Who was he with? What did he eat? Why doesn't he tell me the truth?!*

The more time I spent in my lonely marriage, the more I realized that fighting Grander didn't help. I had begun to imagine Jesus sitting at the dinner table with me when Grander wasn't there, holding his place until he got out of his funk. I wanted to share my beautiful day with him, but he couldn't do the same without revealing his lies.

A wall went up between us. I tried to break it down, but it only pushed Grander away. So I left it there, hoping he would one day want to cross it.

Despite him already being away from home all the time, I had been forcing him to attend Alcoholics Anonymous meetings. He hated going, though, and one day he let the truth burst out of him.

"I'm not an alcoholic!" he announced. "I do drugs!"

I was shocked at first, of course, but suddenly everything made sense—how easy it had been for him to quit drinking, all his complaints about not being able to drink "like a normal person," the late nights working, the bloodshot eyes...

Well, now I knew: he'd only used alcohol as a cover-up for the drugs. It was nice to hear the truth, as devastating as it was.

I was naive and didn't know what to do, so we started attending couples therapy through our church. That was the wrong thing to do. The pastor had good intentions, but he was ill-equipped to handle drug issues. Looking back, my advice would be to first seek psychiatric medical care and rule out any underlying mental health conditions before bothering with couples therapy.

In fact, couples therapy should be the last thing you do, and it should be done well into recovery. When you and your spouse get into couples therapy, it's to heal the wounds and bring you closer together, but you cannot be one with someone who's still actively engaged in addiction. It's physically and spiritually impossible. They may need detox, rehab, personal therapy, medication, a new job, new friends, or even a new environment.

My husband used to say to me, *"Tu eres mi media naranja,"* which means "You are my other half of the orange." It's a sweet saying, but rarely do two half people make a healthy whole.

Do the work on yourselves separately. It will make coming together a lot easier.

CHAPTER TEN

rehab

I WAS ALWAYS A HOPELESS ROMANTIC—HOPELESS, BECAUSE NO matter how hard I toiled, romance never seemed to do me any good. Girls like me fall in love with guys like my husband, and guys like my husband don't treat girls like me with respect. I was too trusting. Too polite. Too insecure. A hopelessly romantic doormat.

Much transpired over the next few months, but when Grander went to treatment for his drug addiction, I promised to be different. I planned to fill my head with movies about independent, career-driven women. Melanie Griffith, here we go.

Becoming a fierce, independent woman was a new feeling for my boy-crazy, poufy-dress-dreaming heart, but somehow, someway, I was going to become one. When I did, I would conquer New York with my newfound independence.

I started by being thankful for what I did have—my boys. I hadn't expected to have sons, but oh boy did I ever love them. I welcomed their laissez-faire chaos, as it was a welcome distraction from my troubles. Boys love their mamas. It's a special relationship I can't explain.

Because I was such a girly-girl, I'd naturally thought I would have a daughter, a little girl who inherited her mother's fire-coloured hair and Irish temper. I would take my daughter shopping for matching designer outfits. We would go to the salon together and get our hair blown out, then finish our day with a meal in a fabulous garden restaurant with fairy lights and tea served in vintage teacups.

When I close my eyes, I can almost see her. She's standing in a wheat field in a long-sleeved white lace dress. Half of her bright red hair is tied back with a black ribbon. She's facing away from me, looking towards the sun. She stretches out her arms to Jesus, and I know she's smiling. She turns her head to the side as if to glance in my direction, but then she runs as though playing tag with a friend. Finally, she stops running and looks at me. Her hair gently falls around her face, her steely eyes see into my soul, and then she smiles. Her freckles alight with glee. With a swish of her hair, she's gone.

While my husband was in rehab, I knew my boys depended on me to raise them alone. My brother came to stay with me for a while to help me through the transition phase of living like a single mother again, and I was glad to have his help. My brother was surprisingly good at domestics. Not only could he cook, as he had been working as a chef, but he did laundry, cleaned, and even changed diapers.

His help gave me time to reflect on what I was going to do moving forward. I spent a lot of time in my Bible. I dug deep into lessons I'd learned in church as a child and had taken for granted. Through journaling, I unearthed my previous love for writing. I picked up my laptop and for the first time in a long while I started to write again.

I became obsessed with learning how to write screenplays and watched hours of YouTube videos. I wrote a screenplay. Then I started writing this book.

I wasn't sure if my writing was any good, but I was overwhelmed with a passion for putting pen to paper—or rather, fingers to keyboard. I didn't think it would be a viable career, but in New York, any dream was possible, right?

I saw that writers could make money by entering writing contests. Lacking formal writing education, I figured it would be a helpful addition to my future resume. In my research, I found a contest for Canadian citizens hosted by an organization called The Word Guild, and they were accepting entries from unpublished authors. There was no cash prize, but they had a mentoring program.

I figured it wouldn't hurt to send in my work and see if it was any good. If it wasn't, I would set aside my pipedream and go back to doing hair. I also prepared my screenplay, ready to start a completely new path in life.

But I didn't enter the contest, for fear of rejection.

My brother went home shortly before my husband returned from his thirty-day program, and we began a new path in our marriage, one full of group therapy, personal counselling, marriage counselling, doctors, drug testing, and twelve-step groups.

When Grander first came home, we were overjoyed to be reunited. As we dug more into what had transpired between us and brought to light past secrets, however, the wall returned. We fought a lot.

My husband was sober-ish, to my knowledge, but he was very angry for what I had "made him do" by going to rehab. He had drifted away from his closest friendships, and looking back I can see that he felt alone. He wanted to go back to the happy life we'd had before all the drug use as much as I did, but we couldn't find our way.

It was painful to have someone I loved be so close and yet so far away.

I have a vivid memory of something I once saw scribbled on a bathroom stall in a rundown music bar: "I'll run from you for the rest of my life." I've always wondered what the writer of this note was running from. Was it a bad relationship? An addiction to drugs or alcohol? Was she running from the demons around her, or the demons within herself?

I wondered if she'd ever escaped. I wanted to tell her that what she ran from could make her stronger. "Look how far you've come!" I'd say. "Eyes ahead! You can do this! You're a survivor!"

In the book of Matthew, Jesus says that following Him and surviving the schemes of the devil is challenging: *"How narrow is the gate and difficult the road that leads to life, and few find it"* (Matthew 7:14). Addiction is no different; some will run from it for the rest of their lives, others won't escape its grip, and some people will give in because it's simply too hard.

How we choose to handle the adversity we face has eternal consequences. Do we turn away, deny, hide, or even run from the things God wants to develop in us? Or do we accept these things and say, "Lord, I'm not strong enough to handle this on my own, but I'm going to face it and do everything you ask me to do anyway."

If we don't cling to love, we run the risk of losing it; a new girl will come along and kiss the boy.

I don't believe it's a godly response to give up on someone battling addiction, but letting go and giving up aren't the same thing. Our loved one's addiction can pull them away from us to a place where only our prayers are able to find them. There may be a period where two people need to live separately to protect the innocence of young children or their mental health. But living in separate homes doesn't mean giving up.

I would dare to say that divorce isn't always giving up, either; only you and God know your prayers. If your spouse chooses to leave you for good, you'll have the satisfaction of knowing that you did all you could. No matter what happens, don't lose yourself with them.

If you love someone in a fight with the demon of addiction, give them over to God. If they come back to you, beautiful. If they don't, know that they're still running from whatever it is that's haunting them—so much so that they may be compelled to write about it on a dirty bathroom stall.

CHAPTER ELEVEN

anxiety

When my husband was in recovery, he sometimes complained about my "insecurity." I know now that it was a ploy to take the heat off himself, but I would dwell on his comments and spin into a never-ending spiral of marital doom.

Does he not like talking to me anymore? Does he wish he had an easier relationship? Hispanic women are super sexy. Way sexier than me. I barely have a chest. Maybe he's just sick of me. He must be getting his fill somewhere else. Is there a cute woman at his work? She gets out of her sweatpants every day because she has a job. That's nice. I would have a job, too, if I hadn't been raising kids for the last decade. I would wear real pants. Maybe even a dress now and then. Maybe she's a supermom who has kids and has still built a career. Well, you know what? She probably has a more supportive husband than I do. Mine works all the time. He's never home. Maybe if he helped me more, I could have a life, too. I would put on a nice skirt, get my nails done, and someone from my workplace would definitely flirt with me because even after two kids I still look great. Well, aside from my chest anyway. The kids ruined it. That's fixable with enough money. Maybe that's the problem. Maybe he likes women with big boobs and money, and he's just not attracted to me anymore. He must not love me anymore. Maybe he never did.

All that from one comment!

Men, take note.

It was worse than that, though. As with most things in life, our reactions to what someone else says or does tells us more about ourselves than them. On top of the insecurity, I also had debilitating social anxiety. The more chaotic my life became with my husband, the more I hermitted.

A writer with social anxiety? No. Never! Yet another cliché.

In those six months he spent in recovery, with the amount of time I had on my hands hiding in my apartment to avoid social interaction, I should have written a hundred books. But my anxiety extended into my newfound career goals and I couldn't finish anything. I'd start writing and stop, commit and abandon, losing all confidence in the stories and my ability to tell them. I didn't think anyone wanted to hear what I had to say. My husband's addiction provided never-ending emotional angst to write about, but who would want to read that?

At the rate my dreams were disintegrating, if I was lucky I might get one article published in *The New York Times* one day. The headline would read "Body of Failed Writer Found Floating in Hudson River."

Self-esteem and self-confidence aren't about *what you see* when you look in the mirror; they're about *how you feel* when you look in the mirror and how much you care about how others perceive you. Who do you think you should be, and what's stopping you from being that person? That's where the problem lies.

Real security is found in having self-esteem and self-confidence in who we are to God, and caring more about His point of view than anyone else's. The second we become inauthentic to ourselves, we lose a piece of who God created us to be. We put up a wall between ourselves and our Father, stifling the creative work He completed in us.

For example, I thought I was pretty, but didn't feel like a sexy Latina, which is what I thought my husband found attractive. I lacked self-confidence in my overall attractiveness to him, which in turn brought down my self-esteem.

This doesn't mean I didn't like who I was. I didn't want to be sexier. I liked being cute, and I knew I would age slowly.[6] I liked my hair colour, freckles, and frame made of tiny but strong Irish bones. I wanted to be myself!

---

6   I call it ginger-retribution, for all the years we gingers spend as awkward children!

But I believed the lie from Satan that my husband would like me more if I were someone else. Someone taller. Boobier. Lippier. If not darker, then blonder. Have you ever believed the lie that you were supposed to be someone else? Better yet, do you even want to be you?

During my husband's recovery, I attended quite a few church conferences. Though I didn't want to expose myself to all those people, I desperately wanted to receive prayer over my family. Many times, the pastor or intercessor told me I needed to know how much God loved me. I figured they had nothing else to say; God wasn't telling them anything, so they said the most generic statement, "God loves you."

Gee. Thanks. Ground-breaking revelation.

One random day, something clicked. They didn't say, "God loves you." They said, "You need to know *how much* God loves you." Knowing something in our heads isn't the same as knowing it in our hearts. Even though I'd become a Christian when I was seven, I don't think I really knew God loved me until I was in my late twenties.

The revelation that God had created me to be the person I was, and not the person I assumed my husband would prefer, blew me away. Me? This unsexy, socially anxious, acne-prone, fiery-tempered, unsuccessful girl? Why would He make such a mess?

God is so much more interesting than we give Him credit for. As Christians, we may not feel like we're the life of the party, but the Holy Spirit lights up the party inside us.[7]

God created humour. He loves to laugh! God likes laughter and joy so much that He gave laughing healing and mood-boosting properties that can temporarily relieve physical pain. In fact, look at all the ways our bodies can heal themselves! You'll discover an aspect of the character of God there.

If you still don't think God is fun, remember that God also created sex. He made it so important that we have to do it in order to sustain human life. There are few things on earth that bring more pleasure and health benefits than sex. You can thank our very quirky, fun, laughing, internal party-lighting Father in heaven for that!

---

7 Eyeroll, much? I admit, that was a super lame thing to say. Even if it's true!

Both men and women embody the nature of God, although in different ways. Men are generally physically stronger and more logic-oriented, while women can be more intuitive and nurturing. I believe that when a married couple works together, both following the direction of the Holy Spirit, they embody a more complete picture of who God is.

By creation, God made your spouse your *media naranja*.[8] In His infinite wisdom, He created us in such a way that we need one another to be complete.

When addiction comes into a relationship, it damages the foundational oneness of marriage. Addiction is a demonic spirit sent to drive a wedge in God's perfect design.

The ultimate goal of the enemy is to break down our relationships, because relationship is what God created us for. The enemy knows this, so he attempts to isolate us, disconnecting us from our spouses through stubborn opinions or a need to be right. He may use anxiety, insecurity, or fear to keep us confined to our safe spaces. He may cause us great pain so we erect emotional walls to protect us from getting hurt, although those walls only hurt us more in the end. Satan may also use false idols, like work, to create breakdowns in communication.

> The ultimate goal of the enemy is to break down our relationships, because relationship is what God created us for.

Long story short, Grander could have married someone else, but he married me. If he had wanted a lippier, boobier, taller wife, he could have found one. He'd spent his whole life around gorgeous women like that.

He loved me as I was.

I realize looking back that God didn't create the parts of myself I wasn't proud of, like my anxiety and insecurity. Satan was messing with my relationship. I viewed what was happening to me selfishly, forgetting that Satan was trying to take us down. If I had seen things clearly, I would have realized that Grander was deflecting his pain, not trying to push me away. Instead of thinking he didn't love me, I would have seen that

---

8   A Spanish saying for soulmate.

he didn't love himself. He felt like *he* wasn't the husband I wanted or deserved. To make matters worse, my actions didn't show him otherwise.

> *Let all bitterness, anger and wrath, shouting and slander be removed from you, along with all malice. And be kind and compassionate to one another, forgiving one another, just as God also forgave you in Christ.*
>
> —Ephesians 4:31–32

I felt God calling me to forgive my husband, and so we started to heal. Then, one week before our anniversary, he relapsed.

CHAPTER TWELVE

canada

My husband's relapses weren't always dramatic. He would just come home looking high and we'd get into a fight. After a while, the pattern became blurry and repetitive. And exhausting.

After the relapse, I was determined not to fall into the same pattern I had been in before, the pattern of being angry and passing blame. I wanted us to heal and felt God strongly pressing on my heart to forgive him.

My mom and dad came to stay in New Jersey for a visit, and afterward the children and I planned to go back to Canada with them to visit family and friends. Grander would join us on the weekend and drive us back home. He couldn't get the time off work for a full holiday.

This was something we did often, but I was nervous to go this time because of the relapse. My mom convinced me that worrying about Grander wasn't a healthy way to live, and I couldn't do anything to solve his drug problem anyway.

On the night of our anniversary, my parents watched the boys so Grander and I could go out on a date. We rarely went out alone, so it was a special treat to go out for the evening. We went to an upscale restaurant in Englewood Cliffs on the Hudson. A jazz band played in the background; nothing embodies the heartbeat of the city like New York jazz.

You have to understand that although we lived in New Jersey, our lives were engrossed in New York. My husband worked there, we shopped there, we occasionally attended church there, and we spent our best days in New York's parks. New York has five official boroughs, consisting of

Manhattan, Staten Island, Queens, Brooklyn, and the Bronx. And our apartment was just as close to Manhattan as any other borough.

Aside from the fact that we technically lived in a separate state, the biggest difference was that our rent was significantly cheaper in New Jersey than it would have been in the city.

Grander ordered the chicken, and I ordered the fish. I despised seafood, but I was trying to learn to like it, as it was healthier than other proteins. The waiter set down our savoury dishes and we shared our dinner in the moonlight. Afterward we took a stroll hand-in-hand along the river boardwalk.

Oh, and then he took me shopping. He sure knew the way to my heart! All was well in my soul.

I went home to Canada for two weeks the following day, thankful that God had been so faithful.

My children and I had a great visit that first week, and there were no major emergencies. I video-called Grander to check in on him from time to time, and he seemed to be doing all right without us there.

The following week, he worked long hours and we didn't have as many calls. On the day he was supposed to drive up to meet us, he left late in the day because he'd been working the night before. I waited for him to arrive. By my calculations, he should have arrived by dinner time.

Hours passed, and still no Grander. I put his dinner in the fridge and hoped he hadn't gotten into an accident. He finally called and explained that he had stopped to eat and would arrive at my parents' house shortly.

Around ten at night, he still wasn't there. The kids were in bed and I was getting more upset as each hour passed. I tried to think positively and hope for the best, but I knew something was wrong.

Grander finally arrived after midnight, and my heart sank when I saw him. Remember when I said that I would be swept off my feet only to hit the floor many times? This was one of those times.

"You look horrible," I said.

He didn't make eye contact. "I'm just tired."

"Grander, did you do something?" I asked, trying to be kind and understanding.

"No, I'm just tired."

He sat down at my parents' kitchen island. I asked him if he was hungry, but he said he had already eaten.

"Grander, you look really bad."

"Well, actually, I haven't been feeling well. I think I'm getting sick."

My mother came into the kitchen and observed our conversation for a while before jumping in and telling him he was a liar.

"We're not stupid," she said. "Give us a little credit. It's obvious what you've done. Why don't you just tell the truth?"

"I'm not lying," he said, getting defensive.

"We're not stupid," she said, repeating herself.

We conversed back and forth like this for the next thirty minutes, until we were all yelling at one another. I was crying, my mom was crying, and finally Grander said, "Okay, yes, I slipped up. But I really am sick."

My mom might not have been dumb, but I was. I believed him. And the next day, I catered to his needs while he lay in bed recovering from his drug use. We got in vicious arguments that weekend under my parents' roof, and I knew he needed more help to quit his habit.

After the happiness of our anniversary, I crashed. I'd had enough.

I emailed the addiction and marriage counsellor we were seeing at the time and asked her what we should do. She suggested that Grander's best shot was to go into long-term treatment, for a minimum of six months. So I started the long and arduous process of trying to find him a rehab spot in the U.S. that we could afford.

We had insurance, but it wouldn't cover a faith-based rehab program. The Christian rehab centres often didn't offer dual-diagnosis programs like the counsellor had suggested. A dual-diagnosis program is one that addresses both the addiction and any possible underlying mental health disorders. So I tried state treatment centres like the last one he had been to, but most people who went there were court-ordered; it wasn't the right environment for voluntary treatment. I wanted him to go to a Christian rehab centre so they could also work towards a spiritual solution. But some of these centres cost upwards of $30,000 per month.

In desperation, I called a Christian centre not far from my parents' house in Canada. I asked if they would take in my husband, because at least I was a Canadian citizen.

They said yes.

Then came the hardest part of all: I told Grander that the boys and I weren't going home with him and I wanted him to go to a treatment program in Canada for six months. For the first time in my marriage, at least to my memory, I lied to him. It wasn't a six-month program—it was a full year, but I knew he would never agree to that.

He was completely devastated. In a second, he'd lost his wife, his kids, and his home, and he could possibly lose his career next. But he reluctantly agreed to go.

I contacted my landlord, hired movers, and rented a moving van. Three days later, Grander and I left the boys with my mom in Canada and drove back to New Jersey with my dad. We packed all our family's belongings, leaving behind only a mattress along with Grander's bicycle, clothing, and computer. He would need these basics when he returned to New Jersey, to finish some work before entering rehab. It was all that now remained of our family home that had once been full of hope and love.

My dad drove his SUV back to Canada, Grander drove the moving van, and I drove home my beloved ten-year-old blue car that I'd originally moved to New Jersey in.

As the New York City skyline shrank in the rear-view mirror, I started to cry. How had my joyful adventure transformed into such a calamitous tragedy? I mourned the life I had dreamed of and spent the next nine hours alone in my car, weeping the whole way home.

CHAPTER THIRTEEN

one year

We crossed the border late at night with very few questions asked. The customs official wondered why I was moving home, and I told her the honest truth: "My husband is going to rehab."

"Welcome home," said the official.

But I wasn't happy to be there.

More devastating than my husband's drug use, the last thing I'd ever wanted was to move back to the place I'd come from. There couldn't have been anything worse, especially after having lived in New York. There would be nothing to do, nowhere to go. No more trendy restaurants or impromptu concerts in the street. No more subway rides to baseball games at Yankee Stadium or trips on the Staten Island Ferry. No more of the European shops found only in New York and Paris. My dream of becoming a real New York writer seemed to be dead.

And I would never eat cheesecake the same way again.

I thought I had hit my personal rock bottom. Denley was just a baby, but poor Beckett had no idea what was happening.

"Mama, when can I go say goodbye to my friends?"

"Mama, what about my school?"

"Mama, what about my taekwondo teacher? He's going to miss me!"

"Mama, why is Papi going back and we can't?"

My husband and I rented a storage unit in the middle of a cornfield. I remember commenting on what a simple business that was to own empty boxes and have people pay you to fill them with their things.

I wasn't sure where we would live long-term, because I had no idea what the future would hold. Our finances were in limbo, I didn't know what would happen with Grander, and I was telling myself whatever lies I needed to in order to keep my head above water.

Grander went back to New York to finish a few weeks of work before heading to rehab. He changed his mind many times about whether he was going or not, and I can't blame him. If I'd had the chance to go back to New York instead of returning to Norfolk County, I would have taken it, too.

In September of that year, I drove him to the treatment centre and said goodbye, once again crying all the way home.

Now that I was living with my parents again, one of my very first thoughts was whether I would run into the Fish. I'd scan the grocery store in fear while at the same time trying not to look for him. I didn't want him to have that power over me.

What if I did run into him? Would I keep my cool? Would I be having a bad hair day? Would I cry? What if I saw him and my whole world fell apart right in front of his blue eyes? My husband had just broken my heart, and I was potentially coming full circle to face my first curly-haired head of heartbreak.

Of course, maybe none of that would happen. Maybe I would just faint.

I'm not exaggerating when I tell you I had all these thoughts in my first ten-minute drive around town. I concluded that I didn't want to see the Fish anyway, and if I did I would turn my back and pretend I hadn't seen him... let him see how nice my derrière had stayed after all these years.

God gave me shelter at that time in my life. For the sixteen months I spent in that town, I never saw the Fish. He was there, but I don't know where. Even so, the hopeless romantic in me still wanted to believe that had I run into him, he would have poured out his heart and told me he'd made an enormous mistake and had always loved me. I wanted to believe this, since he'd been my first love. My first prom date. My first heartbreak.

I wanted to know he had loved me, not because I was still in love with him, but because I had always wondered what it was that had made me so unlovable.

While Grander was in rehab, he and I wrote many letters. Phone calls were limited and visits were meant to be once a month. I thought that was barbaric, so I found out where the group went to church and showed up there as often as I could.

Beckett thought Papi was at a Bible school—and in a sense, he was. The treatment centre was heavily faith-based.

> I wanted to know he had loved me, not because I was still in love with him, but because I had always wondered what it was that had made me so unlovable.

Grander also ran, cooked in the kitchen, and much to my surprise joined the choir. After all this time, I learned my husband could play the drums.

As the time passed, we neared my birthday in November. Grander had forgotten my birthday multiple times early in our marriage, although he would tell you he didn't. That, and he once bought me a pineapple cake. Not only am I allergic to pineapple, but I'm a chocolate kind of girl. The more decadent, the better. I imagined marriage to be more covered-in-chocolate-romantic than pineappley-drink-at-a-college-party, and it took a few years for my husband to catch on.

The treatment centre he went to was on a farm, and I'm pretty sure it crushed his dreams as much as it did mine. However, rows of trees stretched across a wide and open field. By November, the leaves had begun to carpet the ground in their multicoloured splendour. Canadian fall is the best, bar none.

This was the best birthday I'd had during our marriage. Visiting day that month happened to fall on my birthday, so the boys, my parents, and I went together to celebrate with my husband. We all sat at a rickety old picnic table that had undoubtedly heard many difficult conversations. The joy over him being newly sober was special, but even better, he'd bought me a gold bracelet in New York before entering rehab. His friend's wife had helped him pick it out.

Come to think of it now, it's actually quite strange and out of character for him to have shown such foresight. I hope it wasn't some mistress's bracelet I've been wearing all this time! Maybe when he turned from his sins, he left a harlot and bestowed upon me her jewels. It wouldn't have been the bracelet's fault!

But seriously, he normally bought presents the day before. Or the day of.

My husband not only gave me the bracelet he had purchased, he also managed to get a little chocolate cake for the occasion. Every time I wear that bracelet, I'm reminded of how much it means to me. It's an anchor.

All we did that day was rake leaves in the autumn air, jump into well-constructed piles, and play baseball, but it was the best birthday. The thoughtfulness and ease of that day came close to none other.

I went home more hopeful than I'd ever been about our future. The day had reminded me of why I'd fallen in love with Grander in the first place. He was the most fun person I knew, and still know; I love to hang out with him. Even if we do nothing, it will still be the best day I've had all week.

When it comes to relationships, that's the kind of person you want to spend your life with. Someone with whom you find life easy. Maybe it's not easy all the time, because everyone walks through a measure of difficulty, but you want to be with someone like that when everything else has been stripped away. I could be happy with him anywhere, even on a farm in Canada.

When Grander stood to lose everything, he chose to love me, too. And being chosen was the best birthday present a girl could have.

CHAPTER FOURTEEN

recovery

They say being married to an addict is like riding a rollercoaster, and it's not an unfair comparison.[9] Many times during the months my husband spent in rehab, I was up and down emotionally. We had great days and visits, and then we would have bad ones. Because our phone calls were restricted, we weren't always allowed to work things out after a bad day. Once your time was up, that was it. Our fruit of patience (Galatians 5:22) grew very big that year.

The closer our loved ones get to recovery, and the more freedom we find in Christ, the more adversity we inevitably run into. Especially if we're happy. When we're joyful, it angers Satan, who wants only to steal, kill, and destroy our lives for his power (John 10:10). Through addiction, he plans to take down entire families, possibly for generations to come, but these plans can be foiled with joy and lovingkindness.

Freedom from addiction, for all involved, is a process. It doesn't happen overnight. There are highs and lows, ups and downs, and a lot of in-betweens. There will be weeks filled with victory that rejuvenate the soul, and other times when you crash into desolation. Not seeing a way out, a passing thought may occur to you: that it would be easier to drive into oncoming traffic than face another day. It's not suicidal, and you're not even depressed; it's just a reality of addiction.

---

9 I would never call my husband an "addict," but I use the terminology here because I know it's the most common for people to understand.

It's wise to prepare for the attack ahead of time so you can hang onto that joyful feeling in the days of darkness.

If you were planning a trip, you wouldn't go unprepared. No matter how organized or disorganized you may be, you would at least pack some clothing and a toothbrush.[10] You would know your form of transit and have a place to stay. If you're more organized, you may have an itinerary planned with the best route from point A to point B with epic food stops and stunning scenic views along the way. If so, you're my kind of vacay friend!

When it comes to planning recovery, I don't think it's wise to overplan it. God is way more creative than we are. He'll use the recovery process to show you things within yourself that need changing, and use that for His glory. The places He wants to take you may be places no one has gone before. How can you plan for a place no one has been?

God completely changed my plans when my type-A personality had it all laid out: I would graduate university with my English degree and meet a nice boy between the ages of twenty and twenty-one. By twenty-three, he would propose, and after we'd been appropriately engaged for one year we would marry. I would have a child at twenty-five, another child by twenty-seven—one girl, one boy, or two girls—and by thirty I would have my prebaby body back and most of my freedom.

Although my heart's dream would have been to live in an all-white apartment in New York—white art, white furniture, white walls, white rugs, white everything—I didn't believe God would bring that to fruition; the rent was too high. Instead I pictured my future self in a modern home in no particular place.

During the baby years, I would work part-time or own a small business so that by the time the kids started school I could focus on my career while still being relatively young. My husband, of course, would be wonderful with the children.

This plan gave me at least forty solid years of working and growing my income potential. It also ensured that my children were out of the house before I left my prime, so I had money to travel the world with my fabulously supportive husband. We would start our days waking up

---

10 Well, maybe not a toothbrush. That's always the one we forget!

with the sun, then enjoy fresh-roasted coffee on a balcony overlooking the sea. After freshening up, we would stroll down to the water, me with a book, wearing a sleek pair of reading glasses and a white one-piece bathing suit with a matching white kaftan. My husband would carry our beach chairs. And my bag. And the beach umbrella, because he had muscles. Enough said.

If I had known I would move to New York only to have my heart broken and go crawling home to my parents' house, I wouldn't have gone there in the first place.

That's the problem with knowing what will happen; we have the option to run.

The Bible is full of runners. Take Jonah and the whale, for example. Jonah ran away from God and the plan God had for him. He saw the danger and said, "No! I'm not going there." Isn't that how we feel when facing a loved one's addiction? "No way, Jose! I don't want any part of that. God, give me someone else's life!"

The truth is, we can't plan our way out of addiction.

I've been asked many times why I stayed with my husband. I've seen the expression on their faces, felt the criticism. But I'm so glad I waited for God to move. Proud, even. I'm in awe when I think about the beautiful and surprising foreshadowing God wrote into the story when we first met—on New Year's Eve in Niagara Falls, a wonder of the world, celebrating the eve of moving from the old to the new.

There are those who say that leaving an addict is the ultimate way to freedom, but it's not always true. Leaving can bring temporary relief, but it can also leave room for new problems. Running isn't the way to heal a broken heart. If you love them, it will always hurt in some way, even if it's only a painful memory.

Whether we choose to stay in our relationships, we need to heal from them before we'll ever truly be free.

I went through a period of deep anger and hurt toward Grander. When I began to change my own wrong attitudes and judgmental thinking, he came to a turning point. While I learned how deep my battle with insecurity went and how I'd wrongly relied on my husband's love to give me security instead of God's, the veil of bitterness began to lift.

It was during that time that I stopped seeing my husband as an addict and started seeing him as a good but hurting man. And I realized that this experience had been equally painful for him. That last part was the key. The addicted loved one often feels they've made too great a mess and there's no coming back from it.

This is one reason why twelve-step programs work. They break down the problem so easily: do these twelve things and you'll be forgiven and free. They provide a step-by-step process to follow and plenty of peer support along the way.

But the Big Book[11] is not the Bible, and the only way to find real, life-changing, long-lasting healing is through a life transformed by one step, one plan: Jesus.

> *My peace is the legacy I leave to you. I don't give gifts like those of this world. Do not let your heart be troubled or fearful.*
> —John 14:27, The Voice

He's the one guy you can always plan on.

---

11 The Big Book is an affectionate term for *Alcoholics Anonymous: The Story of How Many Thousands of Men and Women Have Recovered from Alcoholism*, the textbook of Alcoholics Anonymous written by Bill Wilson. The first half contains the famous twelve steps of AA and details their recovery program, while the second half is made up of forty-two stories of the founding members who recovered from alcoholism. Members are encouraged to read the book daily and follow its moral guidelines, finding their "higher power." It is commonly used in place of, or in similar fashion to, the Holy Bible.

CHAPTER FIFTEEN

demons

The longer my husband was in treatment, the more I had to confront my personal demons. I tried to find freedom through my husband's recovery and felt that this was the right time to dump my emotional baggage on him.

I nagged Grander daily as he fumbled and bumbled, trying to understand my complex emotions.

"No, you don't understand."

"Can you put yourself in my shoes for three [un-Christian word] seconds?!"

"Never mind! I don't even know why I'm trying to explain anything to you. It's useless!"

He didn't know how to reply, and I knew it. He didn't understand, and I saw it. He felt helpless to fix the damage done to our marriage, and it was unlikely he could have. There were practical things he could have done to address the issues we kept fighting about, but he never would have been able to fix the deep-seated feeling that, at the end of the day, I just wasn't good enough.

This didn't make sense, I knew, but I saw his battle with addiction as a reflection of my personal failure. Somewhere along the line I had failed to pick a proper mate. I thought something within me must have been broken because I continually made the wrong choices.

The same lies came at me over and over again.

"You're a highly intelligent girl who wasted her education."

"You're a college dropout turned single mom who ruined her life in promiscuity."

"You're far from independent, living off of other people. You will never be successful."

I would push these lies away and remind myself that the book of Jeremiah says that God had a great plan for my life. He had a great plan for the Israelites, anyway, and I was supposed to claim that for myself. Honestly, quoting that verse feels like a twist of scripture when we take it for ourselves. God has a good plan for us, but He wasn't talking to us in that specific verse.

Theology aside, my lack of success certainly wasn't due to a lack of trying. If God rewards us in heaven for misguided effort, I will have many mansions.

Take, for example, the struggling hair salon I worked at on commission. I went back to work as a hairstylist while Grander was in rehab, because I knew we would need the money.

I knew going back to work there wouldn't be a financial goldmine, but I tried to find a nice salon where I could make a decent income. The walls of the salon I landed in were painted purple. Really purple. And there were no other stylists in the purple salon, aside from the owner, only an aesthetician.

Something about the place sparked my entrepreneurial spirit, and though working there wasn't bound to be financially lucrative, I liked the owner. I thought, *This is a place I could put love and effort into, and maybe one day I could own my own salon.* So I loved it like it was my own.

Paid on commission, I showed up day after day and worked for free. I helped the owner redesign the salon's logo, made purple marketing materials, helped throw a Christmas party, grew the salon's social media presence by three hundred percent, developed a referral program, and wrote personally addressed thank-you cards to everyone who got chemical services… I worked really hard.

For free.

You may be thinking, why didn't I go work somewhere else? I knew the benefits of working at this particular salon might outweigh the effort I put in, but it would be a lot of work to build a clientele wherever I went. Hairstylists work evenings, weekends, holidays, and early mornings. They're on their feet all day and often don't take a lunch break. It's very hard work and they often start out with very little pay. At best, I could have earned minimum wage working somewhere else. Long-term, it made more sense to try and work on commission, because my earning potential was only limited by my willingness to work.

Except I began to hit roadblocks. The owner wouldn't let me book clients in the evenings because the salon closed early. No evening appointments? That wasn't going to work. I also wasn't able to book anyone late on Saturday afternoons. No weekend appointments? That wasn't going to work, either. The small buds of success from the fruit of hard work began to shrivel.

My clients would say, "I love how you do my hair, but I can't come in from nine to five during the week. I work."

"I know," I'd reply. "I'm sorry…"

You're not good enough, the enemy would whisper.

I've always said that I was the girl who was good at everything, but great at nothing. It's a terrible label to give yourself, but it's always been in my head.

I've always learned quickly. I made my first website watching YouTube tutorials and referencing coding forums. I didn't know anything about Google Analytics, nor did I know what SEO was.[12] I had no idea what I was doing. Did I crash the site a few times? Oh, yes. But I fixed it. A Jill of all trades, you could say.

For a while there, I thought I might like to work in construction. Ha! I think I'd spent too many nights designing homes on 1990s simulation games, but I figured it was like doing very useful artwork.

I've had so many dreams: indie singer, hairstylist to the stars, funeral memorial book designer… how about an interior decorator for funeral homes? This is actually a fantastic idea. Have you ever been in a funeral home? This job is so needed.

And the most recent dream: world-changer through words.

---

12 Search engine optimization. It's what makes your website pop up when people search for things. It's pretty important!

The careers I've mentioned are the ones I more seriously pursued and contemplated. This doesn't include the careers I talked myself out of due to insecurity, like becoming a psychiatrist, lawyer, magazine layout designer, advertiser, actress, or professional cheerleader.

Do you have unaccomplished, unpursued, unfulfilled dreams in the shadows of your past?

When we're called to follow God's radical plan for our lives, Satan becomes afraid. He's been trying since we were children to make sure we never figure out who we are. Do you see how many dreams I had? How different they all were? Satan tried to make a scrambled egg of my future! I doubt writing about addiction was always my life's purpose, but God. You know?

My thought is, Satan can see our unique gifts, talents, and anointing and devises a plan to destroy them. He attacks our personhood, but he doesn't know the future any more than we do.

Back in my parents' basement, facing my past, I learned to be stubborn and rebellious in the face of fear and insecurity. I had to stop running. I had to look the taunting voice in the face and know down to the depths of my soul that it had no power over me.

Satan's destruction, no matter how great, doesn't change who God says you are.

For God has not given us a spirit of fear, but of power and of love and of a sound mind.

—2 Timothy 1:7, NKJV

Power, love, and a sound mind. That's the opposite of fearful, self-deprecating, anxious, or addicted.

"You're not enough" is a lie. None of us were ever "enough" to begin with.

The righteousness of God is through faith in Jesus Christ to all who believe, since there is no distinction. For all have sinned and fall short of the glory of God; they are justified freely by his grace through the redemption that is in Christ Jesus.

—Romans 3:22–24

If you're feeling frustrated in your lack of personal success, take a step back and seek to find meaning in every area of your life. You can fake it until you make it, buy a lot of stuff to make you happy, or win no matter what happens, because you have the right attitude.[13]

I sought the Lord, and he heard me, and delivered me from all my fears.

—Psalm 34:4, KJV

I'm not speaking to you from a place of raving career success. In fact, right now I'm writing on my walnut veneer dining room table, picked up at a yard sale, while sitting on the chair I upholstered in vinyl because, you know, kids. I'll still be happy whether I find success or remain a mom who loves her kids and husband, likes to write every now and then, and sings like she's leading worship for a thousand people while folding laundry. Through my husband's addiction, I found an inner happiness that doesn't rely on anything beyond what's living inside of me.

If you struggle with mediocrity, please understand that all the little things you excel in every day are part of the bigger, more beautiful picture of who you are. Those things aren't purposeless. We all need clean undies, after all, possibly folded into thirds and stacked vertically.

If you can marry the facets of your personality with where you are today and who God created you to be, you're already further ahead than most. There's no crazy secret to life; God wants you to be you. Powerful. Loved. Sound mind. Whole. Beloved child.

Maybe no one will ever hear your laundry song, but as you sing the melody of who you are, you'll bring the light of God's creation into every space of darkness that tries to take up residence in your heart.

It's the kind of success you can't see right away, but it lasts for generations to come.

---

13 #winning!

CHAPTER SIXTEEN

prophecy

Living in the basement of my parents' house made life doable, but we weren't doing well enough to live on our own. I was trying not to be pathetic, so I impulsively spent five hundred dollars on a blogging course.

I'm going to do something, I thought as I slammed in my credit card numbers. *I have to change my life!*

Without a well-paying job, childcare is unaffordable for most single mothers. I would spend a whole day at the salon and make $90 minus taxes, then pick up my kids and pay $67 for childcare. I was bringing home a whopping $20 per day. That was $100 per week, minus $40 for gas, which left me with a $60 per week income. That was $3,360 per year if I didn't take any days off.

It was less than what my husband made in a month.

Tips in small towns can be sporadic. Of course, not all salons are like that, but as I said, the one I was in wasn't doing well. Instead of being lucrative, being paid on commission made things worse. If I had no clients, I would lose $67 per day because I still had to pay the daycare. At $20 per week, it would take almost a month to pay off that debt!

So I decided to become a blogger.

A lot of people think they're going to make big money blogging. We've all heard the stories of that one person who's down on their luck, with no applicable workplace skills, and they become an overnight success as a blogger. What no one tells you is that success in this career is only ten percent about blogging. The rest is all marketing.

I figured I could write about addiction and my faith. But the instructor of the class had her doubts about this topic. A Christian blog about addiction? Yeah, okay.

I wrote three stories: one about being still in God's presence during addiction, one about questioning whether the saying "once an addict, always an addict" is true (it's not), and one about why being a peaceful Christian doesn't mean being a pushover.

I hid my face, changed my name, and used that blog to share things I didn't feel I could say to anyone else, like what God says about disease and addiction and how the two aren't inherently the same.

Over time, my articles got shared more and more, and somehow women found me from all over the world. . One of the first women who joined my online community came from Australia. I received an email from a woman in India who told me she lived in a small and humble hut, but she loved my blog and encouraged me to keep writing. I also got an email from a woman in Africa who told me that she was trying to escape from her husband. The stories kept coming.

I wrote a Bible study to sell on the website and made $400, minus expenses, in the first year. I had prayed God would send just enough income from it to keep the blog going and pay for the website hosting and email server. In His faithfulness, He did.

So I kept on writing. I wrote about how to identify emotional abuse and how to forgive someone who has hurt you through addiction. I wrote the story about why I stayed with my husband, and it was published on *The Huffington Post*. I wrote many articles on marriage and why it was worth the fight, with tips on how to deal with recovery.

Everything I went through, I wrote down.

I didn't make a ton of money, but as God provided, I continued. I wrote about how to pray for peace when you have anxiety and the article was shared over half a million times.

Despite the success, I was still insecure about my writing.

Years before, shortly after Beckett was born, I'd had a dream that I now know was prophetic. In it, I saw a large empty church with wooden pews, much like the community church in Port Rowan I'd attended as a young child. I was looking down into the church as though from a balcony, seeing myself walk down the aisle with Beckett, holding his hand. Then Jesus came out from the wings on the left, out of a stage door. Beckett and I knelt on the carpeted stage stairs and Jesus handed me a pen.

I stood up and the dream ended.

Years before, I'd told Glenna about this dream to see if she could interpret it. She had laughed and said it meant I was going to do great things, but she couldn't tell me yet what those things were. She said that I had what she called "a Joseph anointing."

She said a lot of things that day, and I wish I had recorded them. I remember them from time to time as God wants me to.

While in quarantine in 2020 during the COVID-19 pandemic, I went through an exercise from speaker Bob Hazlett. In it, he said we should ask God what part of His house He would like to show us.

I'd like to share with you what God showed me, because it relates to the dream I had ten years before.

God took me into His art room. The room had no ceiling and the night sky contained the most magnificent colours. As I walked, a path extended down the middle of the room, and I saw angels on either side of it. Some were painting on canvas, some were writing, some were drawing, and others were creating art with textiles and embroidery. A few other angels were lying down and taking the time to dream. I saw others in the corner making music. Many different kinds of music played as I walked by them; the sounds didn't clash with one another, but blended from one to the next like a symphony.

As I walked, a pool appeared in the middle of the path, and stairs went down into the water. I walked in and swam under; there I saw more angels dreaming and creating. I then walked up the stairs and emerged on the other side of the pool, perfectly dry.

When I came to the end of the path, I encountered a flight of many stairs leading upward, and at the top stood an extravagant pipe organ like those in old European Catholic churches. A door behind the organ opened into the night sky and beyond it stars and colours danced in the background. The organ was the conductor of it all, its notes carefully chosen and acting like the wave of a conductor's hand for the entire orchestra of art.

Suddenly, I remembered the vision I had been given many years before, the dream in which I had walked down the church aisle and Jesus had handed me a pen. I realized that the aisle represented my marriage, and the pen was my gift. I had thought Jesus walked out from a stage door, but now I realized He had come from the door of heaven's art room.

Next I saw Jesus standing with me in the art room. I asked Him what gift He had for me that time, and He led me into a separate room. It was quiet here, and a man was writing book after book after book. It only took the man a second before he put down one book and went to the next.

There were many stacks of books in this room—books that Jesus had given people to write but they never had. He slid the stack in front of me and I took one off the top. It was a black book with gold writing, like an old-fashioned Bible.

As He lifted the stack and placed it in my arms, it became clear to me that He wanted me to write all these books. The pile was hundreds of books tall! Jesus then gave me a kiss on the cheek and I found myself back in my room in my parents' basement—in front of my computer.

"Write," I heard God say.

God needs people to write down on paper what He wants to say.

Just like that, ten years later, I finally had the revelation that God had wanted me to be a writer all along. My story wasn't my destiny; my art was. As He had shown me, He would provide what I needed when I needed it. I didn't need to worry about my finances. I only needed to do what He told me to do and He would take care of the rest.

> *Look at the birds in the sky. They do not store food for winter. They don't plant gardens. They do not sow or reap—and yet, they are always fed because your heavenly Father feeds them. And you are even more precious to Him than a beautiful bird. If He looks after them, of course He will look after you. Worrying does not do any good; who here can claim to add even an hour to his life by worrying?*
>
> *Nor should you worry about clothes. Consider the lilies of the field and how they grow. They do not work or weave or sew, and yet their garments are stunning. Even King Solomon, dressed in his most regal garb, was not as lovely as these lilies. And think about*

grassy fields—the grasses are here now, but they will be dead by winter. And yet God adorns them so radiantly. How much more will He clothe you, you of little faith, you who have no trust?

So do not consume yourselves with questions: What will we eat? What will we drink? What will we wear? Outsiders make themselves frantic over such questions; they don't realize that your heavenly Father knows exactly what you need. Seek first the kingdom of God and His righteousness, and then all these things will be given to you too. So do not worry about tomorrow. Let tomorrow worry about itself. Living faithfully is a large enough task for today.

—Matthew 6:26–34, The Voice

If I could have told myself these words a decade ago, I would have spared myself much heartache and worry over what was about to happen next.

CHAPTER SEVENTEEN

alone

They say time heals all wounds. Someone said it, anyway. I don't think it's true. Time creates space and distance between wounds, but the memories still hurt. If it was a particularly bad wound, we can't expect the injury to disappear immediately.

I enrolled my eldest son in Christian school when we moved back to Canada. The school had an open house at the beginning of the year to welcome new families, complete with a free dinner, an outdoor movie, and an opportunity to meet the teachers.

As lovely as it sounded, I didn't want to go. It was a small community filled with nice blond church girls married to nice church boys, and the likelihood of there being other single mothers around was slim to none. There was an even smaller chance of there being a single mother with two different baby daddies. A single mother with two baby daddies and a husband in rehab? Ha! It was almost laughable.

I felt like the scarlet woman. It never helps to be a well-dressed girl with her hair all done up. When I go out like this, other women tend to think I'll be snobby, and they certainly don't want their husbands to talk to me.

On the night of the open house dinner, two empty seats separated me from the mother of the children in chairs nearby. Instead of sitting beside me, her husband stayed standing. As did the husband of the woman sitting across the table, since the seat beside me was the only place to sit.

Welcome to another new school, Leah.

I wanted to be a good sport. I showed up. I smiled at people. I tried to look friendly. No takers. The woman behind me in line for food had talked to me for a blessed two minutes, and I tried very hard not to pull out my phone and be *that* parent. But after an hour of sitting alone at a table watching other people's kids (mine had gone to play), I gave in and read my emails.

I channelled my inner independent businesswoman and pushed away the ridiculous idea that I had to make friends. I was busy and had emails to respond to—important ones, like those announcing the new pencil slacks from a favourite shop of mine and a new fall furniture collection—but in my head, I knew I was a fraud. I wasn't a businesswoman. I barely had a job. What was I, anyway? An abandoned wife, that's what. A beautiful trophy, thrown into a box and donated to the Salvation Army. Wasn't that the most perfect picture of what my life had become?

I had an answer ready if anyone asked where my husband was. I was still wearing wedding rings, after all. I would tell the truth: he'd left for rehab a few weeks ago and it had been really hard ever since. Saying it out loud would be freeing. At the very least, someone might take pity on me and be my friend.

But no one asked.

I know this all sounds terribly sad and pathetic, and I have to admit I was having quite the pity party that day, but there are times when it's okay to mourn the life we wanted. Sometimes you'll be surrounded by couples who say they have issues, even though you know it's not the same. Statistically speaking, at least one other wife at that dinner had a husband who struggled with addiction, but that's not something we talk about at Christian school. It's not something we talk about as Christians, period.

After a lovely dinner, I met my son's teacher. She was unequivocally sweet. I felt good knowing my son had kind people teaching him about Jesus and life all day. What better environment could I want for my children? The school was a *Brady Bunch* blessing from God. I resolved to suck it up and continue on, to put on a brave face.

It was getting dark, which meant it was time to pick my spot for the outdoor movie. I went to my car and loaded myself up with blankets, lawn chairs, snacks, and sweaters. I fumbled to find my keys and lock the car like the paranoid New Yorker I had become, then staggered into the field to find a spot to sit. I'd never locked my doors before I lived in the city—not the car or the house.

I was the only wife I could see trucking her things over. Maybe there were other women there with unhelpful husbands, but I didn't see them while buried beneath my pile of self-pity and outdoor movie necessities.

We found a spot to sit, but then Beckett found some friends to watch with, and there I was… alone. It was a beautiful night. The moon glowed over the movie screen and the warm September breeze was perfect. I tried to look friendly, but at that point I realized it was a lost cause. I watched the cartoon by myself in a single foldout chair, wondering if Jesus might suddenly appear to carry my lawn chair back to the car.

He didn't.

It's interesting how aware we can be of our aloneness, but not of our blessings. This was my new life—not one I was unfamiliar with, because I'd been a single mother when I met Grander, but I definitely hadn't thought I'd be in this position again.

I missed having a husband, but I didn't miss having to live his lie. Had he been there, I would have still felt left out, wondering if anyone else's marital problems were as television-worthy as mine. I would have pitied myself and assumed that none were, all the while wishing I had married a nice quiet church boy and saved myself the heartache of loving this wild New Yorker.

It killed me that my husband had gallivanted all over New York and tainted my childhood dreams. He'd destroyed my favourite place in the world. I hoped I would one day see why God had wanted me back in this position. This very familiar position, in this small town, in this field, living in my parents' basement again.

On a positive note, my life had become addiction-free. I understood that time might never fully heal the wound of addiction, but it would reveal God's goodness.

A wave of peace settled over my spirit as the movie came to a close. I determined to restart my life in this safe place. Scarlet woman or not, I would stay in the shelter of my hometown where my people were. My children would grow up near their grandparents and cousins.

In the meantime, I would continue to dream. And I decided that the next chapter of my life would be more amazing than the last. California? France? Norfolk County? If God could make my hometown a dream come true, I knew in the depths of my soul that He really could do the impossible.

As the emotional twists and turns of addiction so often do, much to my dismay Grander left rehab after completing only nine months of the one-year program and moved back in with my parents and me. I was unhappy that he'd left, but happy to have him home. Plus, I had to remind myself that he'd only agreed to do six months in the first place.

We were waiting for his work permit to arrive from the government, since we planned to stay in Canada. Grander had been offered a good job nearby and our kids could continue attending the Christian school. I may not have married a blond church boy, but I sure could raise one.

As usual, the devil had other plans.

CHAPTER EIGHTEEN

abandoned[14]

Everything was blurry.

This wasn't supposed to happen.

I felt an overwhelming crushing sensation in my chest. I was sure I felt the visible hand of the enemy holding me down.

I remembered reading once that raising your arms over your head helped asthmatics to breathe, so I raised my arms as high as I could and knelt down on the floor. It didn't help. Maybe I was supposed to stand? I stood, arms up. Still nothing. Perhaps I should try sitting? It only got worse.

Sorrow consumed me in waves as I began to drown in my own fear. I couldn't breathe—not figuratively, but literally. I staggered up the stairs toward the bathroom.

Be calm. Be calm. Be calm.

The bathroom was my safe place where I cried all my tears. It was the only place I allowed myself to be sad, where I could look at my honest reflection and tell myself, *Be strong.*

I leaned on the bathroom counter, arms still up over my head, but the demon on my chest continued to suffocate me. I fell to my knees sobbing, gasping, sobbing, gasping.

Suddenly, the hold on my chest squeezed tighter. Panicked thoughts raced through my mind: *I'm going to die! But wait, I don't have a will. God*

---

14 Warning: this chapter contains material that could be a trigger for those with post-traumatic stress disorder and trauma-related mental illness.

wouldn't do that to my babies. No father. No mother. Not today. I will not die today!

I didn't know what was happening, but I knew I needed help. I raced to the phone as fast as I could in my dizzy haze and dialled 911. No idea where my toddler was. No idea where my husband was.

Help. Phone. Focus.

"911, what's your emergency?"

"I… I… I… can't… breathe!"

I fell to the floor, phone in hand as the woman asked me where I lived.

They know, don't they? Didn't I see on TV that they can track my phone number? I need to focus on breathing. Breathe in. Breath out. Breathe.

Suddenly, there he was. My knight in shining armour. I don't know what Grander said to the 911 dispatcher; all I remember is that his hand touched my shoulder and I didn't know where the baby was.

"Ca–ca–call… my… mom!"

Mom would find the baby. Breathe in. Breathe out.

Grander kept touching me and disappearing. Touching me. Talking on the phone. Then he brought in a fan and told me the baby was watching cartoons.

Good. Don't die, Leah. Don't die.

The minutes felt like hours. I was in a strange state of consciousness where I was awake but I could remember only pieces of pictures. It was a sunny day.

I had stayed up late two nights before carefully writing and rewriting my personal boundaries for our marriage, the things I could live with and things I couldn't. I wanted to write the most loving and fair limits the wife of someone struggling with addiction had ever written. I'd planned to have a gentle talk with Grander the next day by channelling my inner quiet blond church girl. Fake it until you make it, right? I had prayed about the pending conversation for days and knew it was the right thing to do.

But I felt he had been backsliding. Not a lot, just a bit. That's how things always began with him—just a little bit. They were small things that wouldn't seem unordinary for the average person, but I knew they could have disastrous consequences for him.

I'll let you in on a secret right now: I was right to be worried. He was no longer reading his Bible. Old friends were resurfacing. He was more and more attached to his phone. He'd picked up smoking again and his attitude was increasingly angry.

None of those would be signs of impending disaster for the average husband. We all go through seasons of closeness and complacency in our relationship with God and each other. But when it came to Grander, every step backward was significant to me, no matter how small. It was just three months after he'd dropped out of the program. Too soon.

When I'd brought up the backsliding with our marriage counsellor, he had suggested I write out new boundaries and have a good healthy chat about them with my husband. And then, just as I was about to talk to him about my carefully, perfectly worded personal boundaries, he blurted out that he was moving back to New York to start work in a month.

That's when the devil placed his hand on my chest and squeezed the air out of me.

My number one personal boundary on that carefully written list? I would not go back to New York. Anywhere but New York. We had discussed this. Screamed about it, in fact.

This was bad. Worst nightmare kind of bad. He couldn't have said anything worse to me in that moment.

I went into fight-or-flight mode. Fearful women don't fight like independent ones; we make desperate ultimatums we aren't strong enough to deliver. I told my husband I wouldn't allow him to drag out my agony for a month. If he was leaving, he needed to do it immediately.

He packed his bags much too easily.

Emotionally, I wasn't ready to follow through on my threat, but in the heat of the moment, out it came. When my husband started packing his bags, calling my chicken-legged bluff, panic set in. I called my pastor. He met with my husband, and three hours later Grander called me and said he wanted to come home. He wasn't leaving after all.

Crisis averted. Take that, Satan!

I slept peacefully. We would have our productive chat the next day, and all would be fine.

The next morning, my husband took my oldest son to Vacation Bible School. When he returned, he said, "We need to talk." After a night of good sleep, because God was so faithful, I was happy to move forward, but my husband looked sombre. I tried to make my own expression look sombre, but I was too excited about our hopeful future and how much he loved me. More than he loved New York, that was for sure. Jesus had won!

I perched on the edge of a chair and watched him say, "I'm leaving. My flight leaves tomorrow. Also, I need $10,000."

I say *watched* because it was one of those out-of-body experiences. I froze in shock and would have stayed that way had it not been for the vice grip the devil had on my heart. The devastation in my heart felt like a roundhouse kick. Where was I? What was happening?

Fast-forward a few hours and I was hyperventilating in my parents' basement.

This wasn't supposed to happen. I had given Grander everything! My hopes, my prayers, my patience, and my most precious, vulnerable love. How could he leave me? How could he choose New York over me?

You have to understand, addiction is never about the substance. It's about the search for happiness, the filling of an empty place in the soul with something that will never truly satisfy—money, adrenaline, alcohol, shopping… It's an endless search to find that which only God can provide. We can stuff ourselves full of these things, tricking ourselves into temporarily forgetting that we're empty, but it's artificial happiness. We get addicted to the feeling of fullness instead of searching for the kind of lasting completeness that can only be found in God.

My husband was behaving like an addict, though he wouldn't admit it. This was a point of contention between us. With his addiction came many learned bad habits: selfishness, a lack of empathy, restlessness, entitlement. Stopping the actual addiction was only the start of the battle. Behaviour modification and recovery was the real war, and I was in the thick of it.

The paramedics came. Mom came. Mom gave me a Xanax. *Thanks, Mom.*

When I finally caught my breath, the paramedics were telling me that I should go to the hospital. All I could think was, *What about the baby?* As if reading my mind, Mom said she would stay with the baby.

But who wants to sit in a hospital bed all alone for hours on end after their husband leaves them? My older son was still at VBS and I couldn't let him come home to hear that his mother had been rushed to the hospital and his dad had abandoned him. I had to be strong. My children needed me.

I signed a waiver saying that I knew what I was doing (I didn't) and the paramedics left. Meanwhile, Grander waited on the front steps of my parents' house for someone to pick him up and take him to his family-less freedom.

My dad came home to watch the baby and kill my husband while my mother took me to the doctor. The upside of coming from a Brady Bunch family is having parents you can always depend on. My parents are great people. If only my husband had been so dependable. Hey, I hadn't wanted boring!

I looked out the window to see what Grander was doing, but he was already gone. Just like that. Vanished into a suburban maze.

Who had picked him up? Where had he gone? Why hadn't he said goodbye to the baby? Or to me? Why hadn't he cared to ask if I was okay?

I didn't have the energy to dwell on such painful questions. I went to the doctor, who enlightened me about panic attacks. Then I went to my pastor, who counselled me on why I shouldn't let go of my marriage. Then I sobbed in the car for a while, put my makeup on, and picked up my son who had thankfully gone to a friend's house after VBS. Some vacation. How was I going to explain this one?

I don't remember how long I cried in the quiet that night, but it was a long time. There was no word from my husband.

The next day, Mom sent in the troops. A woman whose husband had left her a few years earlier came over to have tea and talk. Her son also came to play with the baby. Never underestimate the power of another woman who knows your pain, especially when they bring someone to play with your toddler for two hours.

While she was there, my grandma called. "Has he come home?"

"No, Granny. He hasn't."

"Are you sure? Look at his Instagram. It looks like he's in Toronto. Maybe he didn't get on the plane?"

Hope sprung up inside me. I had prayed that he wouldn't get on the plane! Thank you, Jesus! I knew God wouldn't have failed me in such a painful moment.

I quickly found my husband's Instagram page and looked at the photos my grandma had seen. God bless her, they were from the night before. Apparently, after he'd left me he had gone to a baseball game and taken selfies with all the players.

You have got to be kidding me, I wanted to scream. *That cold-hearted, pig-headed, arrogant, selfish, curly-headed son of a selfie…*

Nope! Don't go there, Leah. Don't go there.

Instantly, I went from grief to seething anger. Breaking the silence, I texted Grander a screenshot of the photos[15] and said something about him being a jerk. He replied that he had gone to the game to make himself feel better, since he had been so upset about leaving.

Right.

My husband, the Latin charmer. *Mi media naranja*, my butt.

Many who have hidden addictions become very good at manipulation to hide their lies. It's quite the artform. The key to success is that the manipulator must believe their own lies. Young girls should be taught how to spot and resist manipulation. Forget about sex-ed and how to put on condoms. It isn't rocket science. In my opinion, teaching girls to spot manipulation, coercion, and extortion would be a much more effective teaching tool for early pregnancy prevention and safe sex, not to mention abstinence! Also, they should be taught about how to avoid getting roofied. But that's a story for another day.

I would do anything to save another woman from experiencing the heartbreak of abandonment. It hurts *so much*. If you've been abandoned, know you are a treasure. Your worth should not be measured by how much someone else loves you.

---

15 Why do we do that? Don't text when you're angry. Hide the phone!

The Father of all creation loves you entirely and without fail. In life's imperfection, even the best man will inevitably hurt you, but if you give God your heart, you will never feel worthless.

CHAPTER NINETEEN

angry

Much to my husband's dismay, as I got into blogging I talked to a growing world of people about their experience with addiction. Surprisingly, despite millions of people suffering with addiction and the effects of it, the majority of average people still know nothing about this. If we broadened the addiction spectrum to include the more socially acceptable addictions, like video games, food, shopping, or electronic devices, the statistics of how many are affected would continue to grow.

Being addicted to a video game doesn't have the same devastating effects as being addicted to methamphetamine—video games can't kill you—but addiction runs rampant in our communities and the vast majority of people know absolutely nothing about how to handle it.

Most people who don't have firsthand experience with the darkness of addiction are uncomfortable talking about it. Or, I'm sorry to say, they pass judgment, saying things like "It's her fault for staying with her husband. If she isn't going to leave, she can suffer the consequences" or "He could get a job if he wanted to. He's a lazy bum." Judgment doesn't need to be spoken aloud to be understood and felt by those involved.

If you want to feel like the scarlet woman, all you have to do is head on over to a welcome dinner for a Christian school as the mother of two children from two different fathers, void of your allegedly reformed, drug-addicted husband who destroyed your life in New York City.

Once at church, shortly after Grander left me, a well-meaning widow approached to let me know how beautiful my children were.[16] She mentioned meeting my husband a few Sundays before and how kind he was.

Have you ever felt as though you can't keep on the polite social filter anymore? I was tired of lying and fake-smiling.

Angry, spitfire, gingersnap words poured out of my mouth. "Oh, well, you probably won't be meeting him ever again. He just left. He moved back to New York. He's not coming back."

"I'm so sorry," the woman replied, fumbling compassionately before recomposing herself from the surprise of my honesty. She laid a weathered hand on my arm. "Don't worry. God can bring him back!"

I stared her straight in the eyes and blankly replied, "No, it's okay. I don't want him back."

Church isn't the place to share such honest thoughts aloud.

The kindly woman assured me I was just hurt and angry and my feelings would pass.

"No," I told her. "This isn't anger speaking. He's an addict, and I've had enough of the rollercoaster. He treated me like crap, and I'm done with it. Good riddance!"

Poor soul, I couldn't keep my mouth shut. And she was right; I *was* angry.

Eventually, my bitter feelings changed into grief and sadness before finally coming around to the same kind of acceptance I had found in the field waiting on Jesus to carry my lawn chair.

That day in church, I hadn't felt up to having that conversation. I was tired of being told God would bring my husband back. How many more times would I believe he would stop hurting me before he did?

Maybe I don't have any faith left, I thought, gravely aware that these thoughts were dangerous ground for a Christian wife. We're not supposed to get a divorce from someone we love. We're supposed to pray that God heals our husbands. If we don't, it's safe to assume we've been called to be long-suffering. But divorce? Never.

---

16 They really are, if I do say so myself!

> *Also, if any woman has an unbelieving husband and he is willing to live with her, she must not divorce her husband.*
> —1 Corinthians 7:13

I imagine if I were terminally ill, I would get tired of people saying, "Have faith! God can heal you!" The reality is that, yes, God can heal, but He doesn't heal everyone; that's why we call them *miracles*. I'm speculating, because I've never been terminally ill, but Christians can be as uncomfortable with death and loss as they are with addiction. Yes, death is sad, but it's inevitable. If you believe the Bible, you won't die and your loss will be temporary.

I used to be afraid of death, but I found peace with it through Grander's struggle with addiction. I knew it was possible I could lose him. Today, I've seen many friends lose the people they love most. It's the separation from those we love we should mourn, not death itself. Death is an end to all suffering, a joyful reunion with Yeshua, and the beginning of our eternity.

It is not death, but life, that is painful.

I believed God could heal my husband. I didn't agree that he was terminally ill with addiction and there would be no cure. Many people say, "Once an addict, always an addict." Twelve-step programs proclaim that those who struggle with addiction must accept "the things that cannot be changed"[17] because they are "powerless over alcohol."[18] No Christian needs to ever utter those words; they're simply not true. God is much bigger than addiction. He will give you the power, love, sound mind, and self-control you need to conquer your addiction (2 Timothy 1:17). You may not win every day at first, but addiction inevitably has an end.

I didn't think Grander needed miraculous healing. I thought he needed deliverance from that sense of powerlessness. He needed to break his chains as a slave to sin.

---

17 "Serenity Prayer," *Wikipedia*. Date of access: August 13, 2020 (https://en.wikipedia.org/wiki/Serenity_Prayer).

18 Bill W., *Alcoholics Anonymous: The Big Book* (New York, NY: Alcoholics Anonymous World Services, 1955), 59.

> *Don't you know that if you offer yourselves to someone as obedient slaves, you are slaves of that one you obey—either of sin leading to death or of obedience leading to righteousness?*
> —Romans 6:16

My husband needed to proclaim the life-giving words of Jesus over himself and say, "I am a new creation in Christ! The old has gone; the new has come!"

Just as God changes our character as we grow closer to Him, the person our loved ones were while they were addicted changes, too. They're not the same person when God begins working in their hearts. It's for the benefit of all involved that we offer enough grace to see them as "new wine."

> *Jesus told them this story: "No one takes cloth off a new coat to cover a hole in an old coat. That would ruin the new coat, and the cloth from the new coat would not be the same as the old cloth. Also, no one ever pours new wine into old wineskins. The new wine would break them. The wine would spill out, and the wineskins would be ruined. You always put new wine into new wineskins."*
> —Luke 5:36–38, ERV

If this is your first time reading anything I've written, I apologize. I'm aware that I just keep slamming the most popular addiction recovery program in the world. While we're at it, we might as well ask, is addiction a disease? Let me counter that with, does it matter? Just because a person has a disease doesn't immediately mean they're a helpless victim.

I don't want you to think I don't have empathy for those who struggle with addiction. I do. I feel immense compassion for the struggle and pain they go through, as well as any underlying mental illness or pre-existing trauma they may have. I don't feel pity, however, on account of their "disease." Everyone has a measure of misery to bear. I don't get to abandon my responsibility to my job, my family, or God because I'm a hurting person, and neither should anyone else. Every day is a good day to change your life!

My husband made the most profound offhand comment once about twelve-step programs. He said, "The problem is that those places, they make it okay to relapse. And sometimes you just need someone to tell you that it isn't okay anymore."

It's better coming from him than me, for obvious reasons.

I always believed my husband would find healing, but I'd been riding the rollercoaster for too long. After he left us, all I could think about was my kids and that it was time they had a chance to live peacefully. If my husband ended up coming along wherever God took us, wonderful. If he chose to continue down his path of destruction, so be it. Jesus was my boyfriend, my most passionate love affair, and He never let me down.

> "The problem is that those places, they make it okay to relapse. And sometimes you just need someone to tell you that it isn't okay anymore."

For each soul who deeply understands what we're going through, there are a thousand hopeful faces who don't. It isn't their fault. I was wrong to punish that lovely lady at church by tearing her kind words with my dagger of anger. If it happens to you and you're in a sour mood like I was, remember that our mothers were right when they said, "If you can't say anything nice, don't say anything at all!"

But—and you knew there would be a *but*, right?—it's okay to be honest, too. Talking about addiction is important. The more we talk about it, the less stigmatized it becomes. There's an addiction epidemic happening right now and few know how to treat it successfully.

If you know someone who's going through this, I would suggest starting by bringing casseroles. An emotionally strengthened, well-fed, and cared-for mother or wife will do wonders to help a husband's addiction. Support the support system.

Have you read about the friends in Mark 2:1–12 who carried their paralyzed buddy to see Jesus for healing? Here's the story—and warning: I've taken some creative liberties.

In a town called Capernaum, Jesus preached the Word of God in a temple. A considerable crowd gathered, and word spread that the crazy man who heals people had come to town. There was a well-known paralyzed man there whose best buds rushed to get him close to Jesus. They hoisted him up on their shoulders on a makeshift cot and carried him to Jesus—probably on a super hot, forty-five degrees Celsius kind of day.

The passage doesn't say anything about the paralyzed man's attitude, but it's safe to assume he wasn't too fond of the idea—because when Jesus healed him...

Well, I'll get to that in a bit.

The friends of the paralyzed man ran him to the temple where Jesus was speaking, and when they finally got there they realized it was too crowded for them to get through. The man on the cot was getting super heavy, his friends probably yelling at each other because one of them was ready to give up, but they hadn't run all that way for nothing.

Not to be deterred from their mission, the men stole—ahem, borrowed—a nearby ladder that no one was paying attention to. The strongest man in the group hoisted his paralyzed friend onto his back and began climbing up the side of the temple. The paralyzed man was no doubt hanging on for dear life; medical care at the time was poor and he would have been utterly helpless if he fell.

At this point, the paralyzed man was not sure he wanted to be a part of this madness. Plus, his hands were getting sweaty from the combination of heat and his nerves.

When they got to the top of the building, the paralyzed man's friends dug through the roof with their bare hands. What was the roof made of? I can only imagine.[19] We all need friends like that!

Finally, they broke through. I imagine that their entry through the roof would have made quite the commotion. The superhero friends then made a human chain and lowered their friend down to Jesus to be healed.

---

19 Actually, someone's already done this research. According to one blogger, "Roofs were constructed from beams covered with branches and a thick layer of mud plaster, though the rafters were sometimes supported by a row of pillars along the middle of the room." (Ferrell Jenkins, "They Removed the Roof Above Jesus," *Ferrell's Travel Blog*. February 23, 2011 [https://ferrelljenkins.blog/2011/02/23/they-removed-the-roof-above-jesus/]).

The best part? Jesus looked at the man and told him he had been healed by the faith of his friends. Not by his own zeal to see Jesus, which is why I'm thinking he was pretty upset about the whole ordeal. Imagine the faith of his friends!

If you have a loved one struggling with an addiction, carry them to Jesus. Believe in faith, hope for them, and pray for them. Climb ladders like King Kong and claw your way through temple ceilings. When you reach a breakthrough, lower them down and let them go. What they do from that point forward is according to their own free will. Like the paralyzed man, they have a choice to pick up their cot and walk away, telling of the good things Jesus has done for them, or they can continue to lay there, stuck in the belief that they're still paralyzed.

I lowered Grander to Jesus shortly after that day and let God have him. Whatever He wanted to do with my husband from then on it would be in His hands.

On this journey, you will meet people with kind intentions who don't understand, but try to remember that in their untarnished hope, they make wonderful friends to carry cots with.

CHAPTER TWENTY

growing

"Nobody understands what I'm going through."

"I understand," says God.

"My friends complain about their husbands, but I would give anything to have a husband whose biggest problem is that he watches sports too often."

"I want to spend time with you," says God.

"You don't know how hard it is to trust someone after they lie to you all the time."

"You can trust Me," says God.

"I'm so overwhelmed. I don't know what to do anymore."

"Let Me fix it," says God.

"God, where are You? Why is this happening to me?"

"I'm here," says God.

I used to write down the conversations I had with God. I don't do that as much anymore, but it's an excellent habit to get into. For one, it creates a timeline reference to look back on to see how faithful God has been to you. Two, it can help you hear God better by removing the religious mud.

I don't know that all my conversations were completely honest and my own voice didn't find its way into them, but as I got into the practice of recording these conversations I began to hear God more clearly.

I believe God is always speaking to us. He's waiting for many of us to listen. He wants to help us let go of our baggage so we can walk in His love and tell people about His grace and forgiveness.

In a painful relationship, there's more to forgiveness than letting go. We also have to make peace with the issues we have with our spouse, be it addiction, infidelity, or something else. We don't lose anything from losing connection. We gain experience. We grow in our testimony. Our character deepens. Pain puts us through a process where we die to ourselves and experience suffering like Jesus. Pain before the resurrection—it's the way God designed for us to experience atonement for our sins.

God will also write our love narrative if we allow Him to. If you find yourself in a difficult relationship, start by asking God if the person you're pining for is the one He would have chosen for you.

While there is a time to fight for love, we also need to be wise enough to let go of love stories we wrote ourselves with great expectation on our hearts. I wrote the perfect daydream for the Fish and me, and it broke my heart when he didn't follow the storyline. I dreamt of a new future before I had my son, and that also went awry. When I met Grander, I felt like God was writing the book, but he, too, broke my heart.

Having free will means I can love the "right" person and do the "right" thing, but they may still choose a different path.

If you're in a place where you feel you need to let go of something—a relationship, a dream, a job—pray and write down what you think God might say. Praying seems so simple, I know. Not everyone hears God well. I know that, too. But trust that God will show you when it's time to fight or time to let go.

Also know that just because something is difficult doesn't mean it isn't right.

A difficult relationship isn't always a consequence; sometimes it's a blessing from God. He's saying, "I chose you for this role, to love this person, to carry this mantle, because you have been faithful. I think you're strong enough to handle it."

Trusting God can sound like a generic, abstract suggestion, but many Christians don't. Let God take everything from you, strip you down to nothing, and then tell me if you still trust Him while you're standing exposed in the street and the devil is stoning you.

Too often, we give in to fear and then do the worst thing we can do: take matters into our own hands instead of relying on Him.

> *Truly I tell you, anyone who will not receive the kingdom of God like a little child will never enter it.*
> —Luke 18:17, NIV

Maturing in our spiritual lives doesn't happen in parallel with our natural lives. We begin as baby believers. Unlike our natural lives, though, this is definitely the longest "era" we stay in. Many never grow beyond the baby believer. We'll go to heaven regardless. Our level of faith doesn't determine how "saved" we are. It does, however, determine the amount of responsibility God gives us in His Kingdom.

God won't give to a baby believer any responsibility requiring mature faith, because doing so won't bring honour to His name. He needs mature believers to rise up and assume roles to advance His heavenly Kingdom here on earth.

At the same time, God loves to give responsibility to people whom the world thinks are unqualified and imperfect, unfit to do God's work. Take, for example, a smoker or a drug addict. They wouldn't be most pastors' first pick to lead the youth group, but that doesn't disqualify them to God.

After talking to many wives of addicts, I feel they have a unique anointing on their lives. God can use their brokenness for His glory—if they radically trust Him and are brave enough to walk on water when they feel they're drowning (Matthew 14:28–29).

They say God is close to the brokenhearted and comforts those crushed in spirit. (Psalm 34:18). Well, I walked around with a broken heart since I was thirteen years old, and I always thought I was alone. No wonder I went from boy to boy, lousy habit to lousy habit, trying to disprove the lie that I was unlovable.

My husband's addiction only exacerbated that insecurity. Interestingly enough, the addiction also prompted my understanding that my life had value. My humble insecurities screamed, "You'll never be good enough!" But God whispered, "I'm in control."

> *When the disciples had Jesus off to themselves, they asked, "Why couldn't we throw it out?"*
> *"Because you're not yet taking God seriously," said Jesus. "The simple truth is that if you had a mere kernel of faith, a poppy seed, say, you would tell this mountain, 'Move!' and it would move. There is nothing you wouldn't be able to tackle."*
> —Matthew 17:19–20, MSG

When it comes to the demons of addiction, we must grow beyond being a baby believer in order to beat them. If there's an area in your life where you're not seeing victory, it could be because you're not yet spiritually mature enough. It's okay, you'll get there.

Keep talking to God. Don't talk to Him like a friend, though, because no one tells their friends everything. Be honest. Super honest, maybe even more honest than you are to yourself, because many of us lie to ourselves about our sin, too. Remember that God is holy. Don't lie to the King.

When you study God's Word and talk to Him, your baby Christian ideas will disappear. You'll increase in discernment and experience God in an intimate and personal way.

When you walk in intimacy with God, He'll let you know if the relationship you're holding onto is one you need to let go of. If He tells you to let go, let go. If He says you need to stay, stay. Cling to Him either way. Mourn the loss of your expectations in God's arms. You're going to be so much happier than you would have been if God had given you what you were asking for.

Been there. Done that.

Be forewarned: the more we trust God, the more the enemy attacks, especially if we start experiencing breakthrough in matters as deep-rooted as addiction. There's no need to worry, because God equips us to handle it. Or He handles it Himself.

When God equips you, you may need to fight. And you might get hurt. It's important to come to peace with pain. Jesus said we would suffer on account of Him (John 15:20, 2 Timothy 3:12, 1 Peter 4:12–14), but we are to rejoice in our suffering because God's glory will be revealed in it. God will not lose, so neither will we.

Most of the time, God will ask you to stop fighting and carry on with life instead. This goes against our nature, because we want to do something, but trusting God *is* doing something! Stop nagging, stop spying, and focus on what's in front of you each day while He takes care of the heart problem in addiction. It won't make sense to the world, but it works.

Did you know that women who are married to men with addictions are a bit like bees? Why a bee? Because science says it should be impossible for a bee to fly, and yet it does. Its little wings carry more weight than they should be able to, but they still complete the daily tasks of everyday living. Bees are busy and heavy-bottomed, and their tiny wings don't keep them down. Bees defy science to pollinate flowers, support the ecosystem so beauty can grow, and make delicious, nutritious honey to boot. Yet we hardly notice they're there until we get too close to them.

This is the wife of an addict. She carries on with her heavy burdens, despite all odds. She works hard to make a living and maintain her hive. She spreads sweet nectar to others but wishes someone would give her some, too. She goes unnoticed, no one seeing her daily pilgrimage, until she buzzes in someone's ear, or stings them because they got too close and they're reminded she's there.

Oh, and how does the bee fly? It creates tiny hurricanes under its wings that move it along. They're lifted by a storm. If you think about it, this is similar to the way God uses adversity to lift us up. We're propelled into our calling by the winds in our lives. These storms, these hurricanes, activate us, mobilizing and releasing us to become the people God made us to be.

Kinda miraculous, don't you think?

The family members affected by addiction are often overlooked when it comes to grief and illness. Our pain is vastly overshadowed by the person engaging in their addiction. After all, no one brings you a casserole when your husband goes to rehab.

I can't help but wonder, with their heavy burdens and busy schedules, if the bee feels like it's flying or just... surviving.

CHAPTER TWENTY-ONE

no

Grander wanted me to move back to New York with him. I didn't want to. In fact, I did everything I could to fight against it. I updated my Canadian license and looked for a new job in Canada. I got preapproved for a mortgage, too. Well, my parents were preapproved, but my name was on the title and I was going to pay the mortgage! Great credit, small income. The plight of a single mother.

I thought my husband had left me. I was one hundred and ten percent sure he'd left me. He was so angry that he'd packed his bags—and even bought himself suitcases, because he didn't have enough bags. It's serious business when you buy yourself a suitcase. He rented himself a room in New Jersey and flew away on an airplane. No goodbye. No post-leaving phone call.

That seems like someone who intends to leave you, does it not?

Living in my parents' basement on the cusp of my thirtieth birthday, I was abandoned with two kids. I let out deep, deep, self-pitying sobs.

During that time, I remember reading the story of Elijah in 1 Kings 19. I could relate to this story! Here's the breakdown: Elijah was a prophet and people didn't like him, so they killed all his friends and then decided to kill him, too. Easy enough, right? So Elijah became afraid and ran away into the wilderness.

Okay, maybe I couldn't relate *exactly*, but that was the depth of self-pitying I was in. I ran right to my parents' basement—not once, but twice. No, three times. Actually, a lot of times. Love you, Mom and Dad!

Back to Elijah. He was afraid, running, and super tired, so he stopped to rest under a forlorn tree. At least, I assume it was forlorn. In my head it looks bleak and deserty, and there's this one lonely tree with hardly any branches or shade… the kind of tree where you're not really shaded at all, but it's your only option. Elijah slumped under this shadeless, orphaned tree in despair. Exhausted, anxious, probably starving, he cried out, "God! Take me now! I can't live another day like this." He wiped a hand dramatically over his forehead to clear away the sweat from his brow.

In the Bible, it reads as though Elijah was suicidal, and maybe he was, but from one runner to another: Elijah, man, I get it. I'm sure you get it, too. Sometimes there's *too much* to deal with. Too much overwhelming you. Too much fear. Too many things coming against you and piling up, one by one, until you finally just want God to take you home. There, someone sweet and wise will braid your hair while you have a good cry and eat heaven-worthy chocolate. Then you'll go dance in a white dress under the rays of sunlight and not have to worry anymore.

That's how I felt after my husband left.

I've been through my own degree of trauma. It's not the worst story *at all*, and I feel like I've lived a privileged life and don't take it for granted. But I also know how it feels when life crashes into you full-speed.

After my husband left, I felt like every day had a new mood. One day I'd be finding my independence, and the next I'd be ready to pack it in. I later heard my mother tell Grander that she hadn't been sure I would make it out of mourning—or my sweatpants. I'd poured much effort into our relationship only for him to crush my heart.

One more point for the curly-headed heartbreakers. One less for Leah.

Much like Elijah, I ran into my own emotional wilderness, dramatically throwing up my hands and proclaiming, "Lord! I can't take this anymore!" I didn't want to die. I was done with the fear, the pain, and the running.

After three weeks in sweatpants, I was ready to wear real pants again. Real pants make me happy. So do cashmere sweaters and merino wool scarves! How could you not be satisfied when your body is snuggled in fluff? Smooth hair, fluffy sweaters, and ginger-shaded eyebrow pencils are the recipe for my happiness.

Elijah cried out to God and went to sleep, maybe hoping he would never wake up. Perhaps he hoped for a comfy new tunic made of spun silk. I don't know. But then an angel of the Lord appeared and touched him. The angel told him to eat, and beside him appeared magical food and refreshments. He ate and went back to sleep—after being touched by an angel; that's some serious depression. Then the angel came back and told him it was time to eat again, but this time the angel added that he had to eat because the journey he was on was "too great" for him.

Can you relate? Is the journey you're on too difficult for you? Eat, friend!

When I thought about following Grander, my insides screamed no! Not a chance. Not happening, ever.

We were barely speaking at the time. The more I thought about moving back to New York, I went from being depressed in my sweatpants to pure anger. Blood-boiling, bone-crushing, revengeful spitfire ginger anger.

Also, I found out that my husband bought himself a new car. An ego car. He doesn't read books very often, so if he ever gets around to reading this, I can assure you he'll roll his eyes in irritation about my mentioning it. I hated that car, and I don't use that word out of context. It was a constant reminder of how he had left me. Every time I saw a picture of it, I was reminded of how little he cared about what he'd done to me and the pain I felt.

He didn't want the kids in his new fancy car for fear they would ruin it. I mean, he's fifty percent their parent, too, so the kids should be allowed to destroy his car fifty percent of the time.

It didn't help that I disliked my own vehicle. My beloved hatchback had decided the journey it was on was too great for it as well, and so it gave up trying. It was suitable for a single person, for a college kid, and not for a mom with young children.

In the middle of the Canadian winter, my car refused to start. Again. And again. It got to the point where I had to leave it plugged into the battery all night for it to start in the morning.

One day, I boosted it and took it to the repair shop for an oil change. The technician there told me that it needed some work—more work than the car was worth to me. Sentimentally, it was priceless. But practically, it had an expiration date. Meanwhile, my mother and father were telling me I needed to get a new vehicle. A safer vehicle.

At the time my car died, Grander had just begun his one-year treatment program, so we couldn't afford a car. I was barely scraping by at the salon, and his disability payments were about to run out.

While in the waiting room of the car shop, I got bored and wandered around the salesroom. I knew I couldn't afford these new vehicles, but it didn't hurt to browse.

I left the salesroom the owner of a brand-new car. Saw that coming, didn't you? It wasn't a fancy car. It had no leather. No sunroof. No upgrades. No bells and whistles. In fact, it was the second cheapest car in the entire shop—the cheapest being the newer version of the car I had already been driving. My new car wasn't high-end, but it would start, and I could almost afford it on my measly income.

Before Grander had gone to treatment, we'd planned on getting me a new car. I needed it. I'd had my eye on a luxury station wagon, which was cooler than a minivan and still big enough to be practical. My son's hockey equipment would fit in the back right next to the stroller, no problem.

Coming from modest roots, no one in my family had ever driven a luxury car before. Still hasn't, actually. I felt spoiled thinking about this station wagon. Much like I had when I'd first started dating Grander. At the time, he'd told me he was buying a Lexus and I could drive it around while he was at work because he wouldn't need it during those hours. I pictured myself driving around New York City, Grace Kelly-style, feeling fancy. He didn't end up buying one.

So now, two days after he abandoned me and returned to New York, I saw his new car on Instagram—and it was the same make as that station wagon I'd wanted.

Really, Lord? I thought. *How patient and forgiving can one woman be? They killed people in the Bible all the time, didn't they?*

Elijah's food from the angel lasted him forty days and nights. It didn't last forever, but take notice that God gave him time. I would imagine this time was needed for Elijah to build his strength and work through his insecurities.

At some point, Elijah left his forlorn tree to hide in a cave. He was still afraid. He didn't want to hurt anymore. He was tired of running, tired of feeling like a pile of poo.

Then God told Elijah to go stand on the mountain. In my imagination, Elijah stood on the edge of a large rocky overhang, the kind of rock that makes a great running board for jumping into the ocean. Perhaps he looked to the sky, tears streaming down his face, and thought, *Lord, I want to obey You, but I cannot bear another day.*

God responded by sending a wind so strong that it broke the rocks on the mountain. As Elijah sought shelter, God sent an earthquake. Then a fire. The world was literally falling down around poor Elijah, regardless of his suicidal tendencies. Life couldn't have gotten worse at that point.

Then, in the smallest, stillest voice, God whispered, "Elijah, why are you hiding?"

Elijah knew His voice and emerged from the cave.

There are times in our lives when it feels like things can't get worse—until they do. Our faith, shaken. Our lives, burned. Our escape, nowhere to be found.

God knows us better than we know ourselves. The first time I read Elijah's story, it didn't make sense to me. Why, after all that destruction, was Elijah finally brave enough to come out of the cave and go where God wanted him to go? I didn't get it! My first thought was, *That's not a very nice thing for God to do to a man who's suicidal!*

I think I know now why Elijah left the cave; he'd gone through the worst life could throw at him, but God never left him. His heavenly Father had kept him safe from harm. Surely God would protect him wherever he went next.

Like, back to New York. If that was what God wanted from me.

Nah. Fat chance!

CHAPTER TWENTY-TWO

still no

As I said in the beginning, everything about New York broke my heart. Just thinking about going back was enough to send me into a panic. And panic, I did. My doctor gave me medication for the panic attacks, but I was emotionally tortured, frantically trying to find a reason not to move back to New York.

That's when God got me fired. Or rather, let go in the kindest way possible.

Remember the salon I told you about? The one I busted my butt for and worked on commission in? They shooed me out the door with a $50 gift card to my favourite store, a hug, and warm wishes. I wish I could adequately explain how it feels to be let go from a job when you already work for free! There are no words.

The owner of the salon explained that she was probably closing the salon. She didn't end up closing shop. But it was clear that God gave me a push out the door.

Truth be told, I'd been feeling for a while that I should leave, but it was so impractical not to have a job and continue living at my parents' house to work on a blog that brought in no income. I should have known better. Great adventures with God don't make sense. Either way, I had made excuses and kept working at the salon past the point I felt I should go.

I wonder what would have happened had I listened. Would I have committed more time to honing my writing craft while I had live-in babysitters? Would I have gotten a job opportunity elsewhere?

After being let go, I applied for jobs for four months. The right way. I redid my resume, dressed respectably, applied in-person, followed up with phone calls, and went to the unemployment centre.

I didn't get one phone call.

I wasn't unqualified. I had a variety of experiences spanning more than fifteen years. It didn't make sense. I applied to every place I could find from an eye doctor's office to an auto repair shop, basically any job that paid over minimum wage and didn't require a uniform with buttons.[20]

If you ever feel a nagging in your heart from God and hear Him say, "Follow Me. Let's go do the irrational together," please don't ignore it. You'll live to regret it. Remember the story of Jonah and the whale? Disobedience has consequences.

Getting fired—or let go, whatever it was—hurt my ego more than it hurt my bank account. My budget got tighter, especially now that I had a car payment.

When I'd met Grander, I had been doing well enough styling hair as a single mother. The money I made paid for all of Beckett's needs, my townhouse, and even gave us a little spending money. The income was sufficient for us, so long as I was thrifty. I used what I had, didn't waste anything, and saved every gift bag and piece of tissue paper. I shared a satellite receiver with my parents and paid my small share.

Not only that but Beckett attended a reputable French school in our community, so he'd be bilingual. I'll always remember the time he wore new rubber boots to school, ran up to his teacher, and said, "*Regarde! Me nouveau boots!*" I wasn't sure if he'd said it properly, but I was so proud of my blond bilingual church boy.

Life as a single mother is hard. Silly things that don't seem like much can be difficult. For example, those times when you want to have company over but there's no one to help you pull apart your dining table to put in the leaf. It's no joke! Or when you have to deal with the mouse that keeps sneaking around in the basement while your child is scared and clinging to you because there's no other parent to catch it.[21]

---

20 I have koumpounophobia, a fear of buttons. Yes, it's a real thing.
21 True story. I locked the basement, blocked the door with towels, and called my dad.

If you're reading this and you're a single mother, may God bless you in every way. When sitting at your dinner table eating the small meal you made for one adult and child (or children), know that Jesus is sitting at your table occupying an empty seat. He's always been there. He's proud of you and thinks that great big bowl of cereal you made was delicious.

To be totally honest, I have a dream-like picture of that time of my life. It wasn't all blissful, but it was the calm before the chaos. It was the last time I stood on my own two feet, the last time I felt independent and successful.

But then, on a cold and wintery street just after midnight on New Year's Eve, New York walked into my life. It fit into the plan I'd had for myself. Get out of my small town? Check. Work for a high-end salon? There were plenty in New York. Open my own salon? Complicated, but I'd figure it out. I felt like God was lifting me to new heights.

As you know, that never happened. I was offered a job in New York's East Village in a small, high-end eco-salon making straight commission at thirty percent of all services. Thirty percent! The hours were from 10:00 a.m. to 10:00 p.m., and with the transit ride from Jersey I would actually be out of the house from 8:30 a.m. to 11:30 p.m. Who would watch Beckett? Grander was on call back then and worked crazy hours, so I couldn't rely on him. I didn't know a soul.

We once got a babysitter who had been recommended by a friend. The babysitter, unbeknownst to me, took my four-year-old son on a subway ride to her house late in the evening to pick up her daughter—without telling us! I only found out about it later when I thought I was taking my son on his first subway ride and he said to me, "Mommy, I went on here with my babysitter!" Take a guess who else got fired that day.

Fast-forward to the present, and there I was, worse off than where I'd started. I didn't know what God's plan was—it wasn't New York, obviously—but I knew I was turning the page on a new chapter of my life.

That year, though, I kept seeing license plates from New York, which wasn't normal. I kept trying to spot the license plates in my rear-view mirror. I told myself this was just a reminder not to go back there. I should have seen the signs, but I saw what I wanted to see. God even blasted me with a huge message on a billboard. It said something to the effect of "Don't look at what's behind you. Look at what's in front of you."

I refused to get the message, but God wasn't done trying to get my attention.

After my husband went back to the city of sin, after the separation papers were drawn up, he gallantly drove back up to Canada to prove his repentant heart. He asked me to move back, I briefly reconsidered my decision. Deciding against it, I convinced Grander to take a job in Canada and he agreed.

Without any distraction now from my previous job at the salon, I invested all my time in the blog and hoped that writing was the direction God would take me in. I joined a group of women in media, focused on honing my craft, and finished the blogging course I had signed up for. I bravely submitted my screenplay and the first portion of this book to The Word Guild writing contest I had seen so long ago. I was ready to become independent again and grow professionally—in Canada.

One day, once I thought our plans were set in stone, my husband called and told me that he'd been offered an incredible job opportunity in New York. It was the kind of dream job one works toward throughout their entire self-made career and still may never reach. In other words, he couldn't turn it down.

"No!" I cried.

Not there. Anywhere but there.

It was the devil, I was sure.

I spent many days in prayer over returning to New York, but God was silent. He offered no words of clarity or solace in my internal debate. I made pro/con lists, then looked at those lists and saw that I had no good reason to go back to New York, except for the devil's opportunity.

Then, one night, I went outside to bring in the empty recycling bins—a chore I had never done, by the way. It was an ordinary night. I gazed up at the clear Canadian sky, enjoying the pinks and oranges of the setting sun.

Suddenly, hundreds of wild geese flew directly over my head from west to east. They were so close that I could hear the flapping of their wings.

In Canada, we have a lot of wild geese. I've been around them all my life and never experienced them flying so close.

I stood there, dumbfounded, and after a moment four stragglers flew by. Just four. In a perfect quadrant.

Four birds… four birds… where had I just read something about that?

I ran inside to pick up the book I'd been reading, *Dreaming with God* by Bill Johnson.[22] I flipped to where he had talked about the four birds, the guardians, a blessing…

What kind of birds were they? I asked myself as I frantically scanned the pages.

There it was… wild geese.

What did it mean?

Prophetic teachers say the Holy Spirit is represented by the wild goose and the wild goose cannot be caged, but in Canada it's not a supernatural experience to see one flying over you.

Naturally, I asked Google, "What's the significance of the wild goose in Christianity?" The first article that popped up came from a website called The Elijah List. Mind you, I would take what I read on any website with a grain of salt, but God talks to us in many ways. On that page, Kathie Walters of Good New Ministries wrote,

> So the geese are, in many ways, like a small army. And the boldness and wildness that can't be contained is very present. Now, there are many wonderful ministries in Canada that are unknown, and relatively few ministries from there become well-known. There are people like Patricia King, and Todd Bentley, Stacey and Wesley Campbell, Charlie Robinson, Samuel Robinson, and others, but there are many more that are hidden inside Canada, and we don't hear about them.
>
> But God is going to draw back the curtain, and those ministries will be seen, and they will follow the Wild Goose all over the world. They will carry the wild goose anointing. It will flow down into the USA, across the Niagara, and from Quebec and Vancouver. A strong Wild Goose anointing will flow between Canada and USA and Wales and the rest of the UK.

---

22 Bill Johnson, *Dreaming with God* (Shippensburg, PA: Destiny Image, 2006).

A lot of Christians abandon their boldness because they are afraid of being called rebellious, and certainly, that has been used to tame people – and keep them caged – in some places. 'Don't rattle the cage,' 'Don't rock the boat,' and 'Everyone is in place to support my ministry,' has been the thinking of many ministers. But if you are Spirit-led, then you will be unpredictable; that does not mean unreliable and stupid, but that you are open to being led by the Holy Spirit, The Wild Goose."[23]

I lived in rural Canada, outside the Niagara region where I would cross to go back to New York, and I had a small ministry…
Lord, please. No, no! N-O spells no!
"Fine, God," I said. "I'll go."

---

[23] Kathie Walters, "Following the Wild Goose: Prophetic Words for Canada, the USA, Wales, and Whoever Wants to Follow the Wild Goose," *The Elijah List*. April 25, 2014 (https://www.elijahlist.com/words/display_word.html?ID=13359).

CHAPTER TWENTY-THREE

i'm back

AFTER I CONSENTED TO RETURN TO NEW YORK, I FELT AN overwhelming sense of peace and purpose about what God had shown me. I was excited. It felt great!

That is, until I started packing.

One box at a time, the panic came back. *Oh my goodness, I'm packing my summer clothes. What if I need a bathing suit? What do I need a bathing suit for? It's December. Well, you never know. Maybe I need a bathing suit. Maybe I should take the baby swimming before we move, but I don't have my parents' help anymore… Denley would like that. I want to take him, but you have to sign up for a six-week program and I only have three weeks before I go. It doesn't make sense to pay for just three weeks. Three weeks! Oh my goodness, how can I only have three weeks?! Three weeks and I'm back to no babysitters, no freedom, no support. This is crazy. What am I doing? You know, I don't need to pack this right now. I'll leave this box for later…*

I panicked through a flood of memories, each box bringing on complicated feelings and often tears. I wasn't ready for this, but I knew that God sometimes tells people to do things they're not prepared for. That's where obedience comes in, right? Faith in the fire. Good things come to those who are faithful.

So, faithfully and tearfully, I packed my boxes.

My husband, on the other hand, was excited. Very excited. While I cringed in fear, he jumped for joy. It was sad, really.

I was determined to listen to God and not act on my own feelings, but I couldn't make myself feel joyful about this. Each time I thought I'd come to terms with moving, something would remind me of the past and I'd feel afraid again. Peace would come and I would hang onto every last, lingering second of it before it dissipated and left me drowning in fear.

Maybe I would make those headlines after all: "Canadian Girl Found Floating in the Hudson River: Cause of Death Reported to be Insurmountable Fear of Future."

I had a choice: stay in my Canadian comfort zone, safe in my parents' house, or act in faith and take a risk to get what I really wanted. I knew that the biggest reward would come from doing what scared me, so I pushed through the panic attacks and kept packing, one faithful box at a time.

Remember the One who loves you holds your future in His capable hands:

There is no fear in [God]; instead, [our] perfect [God] drives out fear, because fear involves punishment. So the one who fears is not complete in [God].

—1 John 4:18

I don't know how people get through life without faith or real love. I really don't. My faith is the driving force behind my everything—my navigation system and my moral code. I would never have agreed to move or forgiven Grander without God's prompting.

The weeks leading up to my move back to New York were some of the most emotional I've ever had. My fickle emotions changed their mind a million times, but I knew I had to go where God was leading me.

I'd like to be able to say that I returned to New Jersey and life was a dream, that none of my fears came true, and that moving back was the best choice I'd ever made. In reality, after moving back in with Grander I was a mess! I panicked over the smallest things, had intense panic attacks every other day, and I was most certainly *not okay*.

The whole time this was going on, I continued blogging. I showed my face that year and stopped hiding my identity online. I used my platform to share my rawest feelings and found so many other Christians affected by addiction. That year, my blog had more than 130,000 readers. I was sad to know they were out there, but glad to know I was not the only one. It gave me the strength to carry on.

I felt that God had given me a mission, that I was responsible to find the way out of the darkness of my husband's addiction so I could show these women who had trusted their hearts to me what they needed to do. That's always the question: "What do I do when..." God had to have an answer—a concrete, His-kind-of-way solution that actually worked.

> *Ask, and it will be given to you. Seek, and you will find. Knock, and the door will be opened to you. For everyone who asks receives, and the one who seeks finds, and to the one who knocks, the door will be opened.*
>
> —Matthew 7:7–8

As time went on, the pain in my chest lessened—not because I was over the pain my husband's addiction had caused me, but because it was killing me. I couldn't live in a constant state of fear anymore. Until then, I thought I'd known what it was like to feel anxious, and maybe in a small way I did. But never like this.

> That's where I was: back living in a movie-worthy suburb outside of New York City, trapped in the nightmare of my imagination.

There are times when we have to let go of how our spouse has hurt us for the sake of our health, no matter what they've done. It's hard to do, but there is freedom in it. It doesn't mean we don't care about those things anymore, but we will be fine, no matter what happens.

That's where I was: back living in a movie-worthy suburb outside of New York City, trapped in the nightmare of my imagination.

I couldn't stop thinking about what would happen if I had to take on our massive mortgage by myself. I'd had to sell my new, non-luxury car, and I was upset about it. It felt like I was losing my last shred of independence. I was overwhelmed thinking about starting over the hunt for a babysitter, doctor, dentist, and church in a new neighbourhood.

Leaning on my faith, I gave up.

Lord, I begged, back in the fetal position on the bathroom floor, *I need you to help me. I can't do this anymore. I can't keep feeling this way. I want to move past this pain.*

With the Holy Spirit's help, I did. I woke up feeling free and full of love for my husband. I was filled with gratitude and healthy pride over how far he had come in his recovery. I felt thankful for my new home, to be closer to living my childhood dreams. I saw everything around me with brand-new, grateful eyes.

The Lord had come through! I blogged about it.

My husband had a good job in those days and spent a lot of time in the city. He was flourishing in his career and happy that we were home with him. His job had a lot of perks, so he was always coming home with goodies for the kids and me.

I was happy for him, thankful for our second chance, but as time went on I still felt unsatisfied. It didn't seem right that my husband should get everything he'd ever wanted while I was still stuck at home.

At first I couldn't work harder because of the panic attacks. Then it was unpacking, and then getting the kids into school. We signed up my older boy for baseball, and both the boys for taekwondo. There was always something to keep me from pursuing my goals.

I realize this is a normal mother problem, but this was the third home I'd lived in so close to my dream city.

Third time's the charm, I told myself, trying not to be discouraged. Through unpacking, painting, laundry, cooking, cleaning, grocery shopping, homework, therapy, and toddlers, I would find a way.

Every night, I stayed up late writing. Often I wrote until two or three in the morning. Grander wouldn't be home until at least nine or ten as it was, so I had a lot of time in the evenings. I was tired, but everyone in business will tell you the same success story: it took hard work. So I worked hard.

My blog was still growing and I started teaching classes online on how to set godly boundaries when your spouse has an addiction. I also got quite good at making graphics and videos.

I loved writing and found fulfillment in helping women who came to my site, but I never felt like I had enough time. I desperately wanted a babysitter to help me with Denley so I could focus on my work, but it wasn't financially possible. Occasionally, during school hours, I would sit the little one beside me with a box of toys and pray that he played with them for more than twenty minutes. Not long after, he'd stop napping. Gotta love toddlers.

As the blog grew, God sent two women to help me when I needed them most. Together we managed the site, but the way I had to work still left me feeling disappointed.

Meanwhile, every day my husband got dressed for work and went into the city. He needed to think about nothing else but work. Weekly, sometimes daily, he'd send me photos of the view from his building, his tasty lunch, the new friends he was making, and the city events he saw while out walking. Celebrities. Protests. Fireworks. A helicopter crashing into a building on Seventh Avenue. It all looked very alive from where I was sitting. It was inconsiderate of him not to realize I wished I was there, too.

I tried not to be a sourpuss. I told myself I was one of the lucky ones, that in a few years I would have more free time when the kids were both in school. Then I would be able to pursue my career. I should enjoy this time with my kids while I had it.

One day, not an especially unique day, I sat down at my computer and opened an email from The Word Guild. It was about the contest winners that year.

I had won!

I called my mom. "Mom! I won the contest!"

"What did you win?"

"The writing contest I entered, I won!"

"What did you win, though?"

"There's a fancy dinner, and I get a mentor. I don't know. It doesn't matter, I won!"

"What category did you win in?"

"All of them. I won the grand prize for unpublished authors!"

"Well, that's wonderful, honey. I can't wait to tell your father. He's going to be so proud of you! Can we come to the dinner?"

Ecstatic isn't a big enough word to describe how I felt in that moment. I wasn't a loser stay-at-home mother and horrible writer. I was a stay-at-home mother turned talented, award-winning writer! It was the validation I'd been looking for.

Then Grander relapsed again.

CHAPTER TWENTY-FOUR

relapse

It would be an understatement to say my spirit was crushed by Grander's relapse. Despite my blog's growing success, I wanted to quit writing. Who was I to tell people to have hope in God's healing when He so clearly hadn't helped my husband?

What was it going to take for Grander to stop? A heart attack? A car crash? Divorce? Getting fired from his job?

I couldn't do it anymore.

I quietly retrieved my sweatpants from their pyjama drawer slumber and sunk into emotional devastation.

It's been said that loving someone with an addiction is like grieving someone who is still alive but keeps dying over and over again. But that description isn't accurate. Grief over death is horrible and permanent, but it's time that makes grief over loss so very painful. During active addiction, the heart has no time to heal, because each time it does, it's broken again. It's more akin to emotional abuse than to loss. Many women I've spoken to over the years have shown symptoms of post-traumatic stress disorder, and I think this is why. Their wounds don't come from exterior trauma, but from wounds of the heart. Which is why the condition is so hard to treat and even harder to know when the wounds have healed.

God allows His faithful people to walk through adversity and hardship, even when it nearly destroys them. I can't imagine that Shadrach,

Meshach, and Abednego were comfortable in the belly of fire (Daniel 3). Though the fire didn't burn them, I'd bet it was still sweltering.

That's how I felt. I knew I would make it through the fire, but it was terrifying and painful to stand in the midst of my worst nightmare.

How many errors in judgment could one girl make in her life?

Dear New York, you lied to me. You said I was home, but I was far from it. You said I could be anyone I wanted, but I was trapped. Your streets drip with the blood, sweat, and tears of dreamers like me. As a young girl, I lay on the floor of my bedroom and imagined my life with you; I would sing Broadway musicals on rooftops, put on fabulous plays and make the audience roar, and write grand love stories worthy of *The Great Gatsby*.[24] We'd dance your streets, swinging round lampposts in our tap shoes. But in New Jersey, I couldn't reach you. I was bound by my husband's addiction. You were so close, I could taste it—or more appropriately, smell it. Roasted cashews, pizza, and bagels. Subway steam rising through city streets. The heartbeat of the city echoing in the suburbs.

Was this is it for me? Would my story change? If I stayed in my sweatpants, would God give my dream to someone else?

After two weeks of feeling sad—that's a long time for me, I'm eternally optimistic—I did what I always do and determined that God would fix this. He would save me! There was a plan.

I carefully made an official list of what I would do while waiting for God's plan to come to fruition:

1. Wake up early to work on writing.
2. Take the time to enjoy life's little things and have myself a cup of French-pressed coffee.
3. Listen to music that makes me dream again.
4. Meet with God intimately every single day.
5. Give my children the best of me.
6. Stop skipping exercise.
7. Go to the park more.

---

24 F. Scott Fitzgerald, *The Great Gatsby* (New York, NY: Scribner, 1925).

8. Try to find writing jobs to make extra income and secure my financial independence again.
9. Stop focusing on my husband's iniquities. We all have stuff.
10. Start going to regular marriage counselling.

For our sanity, it's helpful to have plans. Routine is good for the soul. In the midst of addiction, it's often all we can do.

There had been a few points in my marriage when I'd been ready to walk away, and a few other points when I'd wanted to run. Relapse was always a time of wanting to run—to put on my sneakers and a big poufy dress and not look back.

Of course, it wasn't that easy. I had children to carry with me, and that would make running much harder. My husband? He could flee, drive away free as a bird in his new luxury car. He had no responsibility except for what the state would make him pay for support, and even that was only for a maximum of twenty years.

Don't get me wrong: I adore my children and would never leave them behind. I'd live in a tent with my munchkins if I had to. But the more children I had, the harder it was to run away from my problems. That's something to take note of the next time you wonder why a woman hasn't left her abusive husband.

After Grander's relapse, I went to stay with a friend. She had a one-bedroom basement apartment and welcomed me with my two children and her two cats. We would be cat ladies, and wear matching glasses and furry sweaters on our family Christmas cards.

I didn't want to go back to Canada again, because I didn't want to keep burdening my family. I was tired of being the one with all the problems, bringing addiction to our otherwise happy gatherings. Besides, my father had told me I wasn't to go back there. He'd said if I chose to move back to New York to live with my husband, I'd have to deal with the consequences of that decision.

Setting his boundaries, I see.

No, I would stay. No matter how much of a foreigner I was, New Jersey was now my home. My name was on the deed of the house we'd purchased, and I liked the authentic Italian deli down the street. The super sub was my favourite. I don't know what Italians put in their oil and vinegar, but it's the only way to eat a sub. Or salad. Or spaghetti. Or pizza. The owner of the deli would shred the lettuce into tiny shards, fold in layers of smoked pastrami and prosciutto[25], then lovingly lay it all on a perfectly crunchy but soft Italian roll, nestled in tomatoes, dripping in Italian oil and vinegar. After eating half a sandwich, I was full, but I'd still have to eat it all. It was too delicious.

No, if everything went wrong in New Jersey this time, Grander would have to be the one to go. I couldn't see myself leaving the deli.

The relapse brought back a flood of insecurities. Time had passed since I'd entered the writing contest and I had still only finished half of my book. I couldn't imagine having enough free time to go into the city to meet with potential publishers, or being able to afford the mortgage on my own. I hated being financially dependent on Grander. Nothing in my independence-dreaming soul enjoyed spending "his" money.

Grander is much more traditional than I am and I think it made him feel good to provide for us. However, his sense of entitlement, combined with my lack of security, set off a bubbling brew of trouble. We were struggling. We'd lost our health benefits while he was pursuing his dream job and his income had dropped. The reality of our financial situation was becoming more grim every day. He gave up driving to work and started commuting. We stopped painting the house. Stopped gardening. Stopped eating out. Stopped buying clothes. Many days, our groceries went on a credit card. When that got maxed out, they went on my other credit card. We couldn't afford the weekly medical appointments anymore to address my husband's issues and our marriage.

We were flat-out broke.

"Broke but happy," Grander would say, quoting me before his relapse… but I didn't feel so happy anymore. I felt discouraged. And angry. And anxious. I was mad at him for bringing the kids and me back to New Jersey. We'd been happy where we were and I'd felt secure there.

---

25 I normally abstain from eating pork, but I made an exception for the super sub.

I felt manipulated. My husband knew just how to get me. He'd tapped into the faint glimmer in my heart where the fire still burned for New York City.

"Move," he'd said. "One day, you're going to have your books in Barnes and Noble."

If I chose to run this time, not only would I be running away from my marriage but I would be running away from the direction I knew God had given me. It was a mission, an ordinance, a gift. When God says that something will be, it is.

There was nothing I could do to derail God's plans, except to run away from it. As Jonah had found out, even that doesn't work. I'd love to know how his story ended. The biblical account leaves us hanging with him sitting under a tree, angry!

> *Then God asked Jonah, "Is it right for you to be angry about the plant?"*
> *"Yes, it's right!" he replied. "I'm angry enough to die!"*
> —Jonah 4:9

Cheeky, that Jonah.

Instead of giving up on my blog, I wrote about the relapse. I shared with the ladies in our support group how painful Grander's relapse was and how deeply it had affected me.

> I am too tired to fight the negative thoughts and too hurt to force hope and positivity. I wanted to give up on everything, including God, and for a time, I was lost in the brokenness of it all. Mourning, yet again. Just as life seemed to get better, the sun began to shine, and I smiled in the darkness, the addiction returned in all its ugliness.
>
> This cycle of hope and hopelessness is the epitome of loving an addict. So here I sit, mourning the return of this burden. Mourning the time spent hoping and wishing that more than anything, God would intervene in my life and pull me out of this place I'm in.

As Zechariah 9:12 says, *"Return to your fortress, you prisoners of hope; even now I announce that I will restore twice as much to you"* (NIV). "Return to your fortress..." It sounds like Zechariah was talking to a runner, doesn't it?

If you're like Jonah or me and feel like running away from what God has asked you to do, return to your fortress. Return to your prison of hope. Because the truth about running is that there will come a day when we're too tired or burdened to run. We have to return to our fortress or be rendered homeless.

Run home. Run to Jesus. Wherever you run, don't run from God's promise.

CHAPTER TWENTY-FIVE

devil car

I KNEW THAT IF I WAS GOING TO TOUGH OUT MY MARRIAGE FOR THE long haul and trust God to use everything for my good (Romans 8:28), I needed support in our new neighbourhood. I spent a lot of time supporting women whose husbands were in active addiction, but I didn't have a network of my own.

Our family started to attend Hillsong in New Jersey and I was determined to get involved with the church. Until that point, with all the moving and chaos, I'd always been too overwhelmed to serve. I'd been raised in the church and my parents had both volunteered; I think it's important for children to see their parents doing that.

I bought a sole ticket for the Sisterhood Conference held by Hillsong every year in Brooklyn and emailed the church to let them know that I would be driving there if anyone else needed a ride. I'd been learning how to drive safely in New York City, which isn't for the faint of heart. It was one more way to solidify my independence.

I gave a ride to two other women, one of whom hosted a Saturday women's group through the church. When the conference was finished, I drove the women home and told them that I'd see them at the group on Saturday morning.

Grander had worked late on Friday and I was worried he'd be too tired to watch the children the next day. I woke up excited to build new friendships. With the recent relapse, I so needed a friend.

Grander successfully dragged his tired butt out of bed to help me, and I picked out a cute and casual outfit to wear, then did my hair, put on my makeup, and got into Grander's car so I could go meet the women.

I was about to turn on the ignition when I noticed a chunk of something that looked like powdered sugar on the gear shift. My heart sank.

I could see Grander watching me from the window upstairs. As I looked around the car, I noticed there was white powder everywhere—on the dashboard, the steering wheel, the seat, and the floor. I licked my finger, swiped up a chunk of it, and went back into the house. Grander met me in the entryway and blocked me from coming inside.

"Lick this," I said with determination.

"No," he replied, bristled and defensive, his eyes darting across the street to see if the neighbours were watching.

"Lick it!" I ordered, angrier this time, without a care about the neighbours.

He tried playing dumb. "What is it?"

As if he didn't know.

"I don't know," I said, pretending to be just as naive. "It tastes weird."

He licked it. "Hmm... doesn't take like anything."

I stared at him, trying to figure out whether he was lying to me for yet the billionth time or I was the crazy one for picking things off the floor of his car and licking them. Unsure, I wiped my hands, spun around, and drove off to the women's group I was now late for.

When I got there, I parked and looked around the car again. This time, I could thoroughly inspect the crevices without him lurking in the window.

> I stared at him, trying to figure out whether he was lying to me for yet the billionth time or I was the crazy one for picking things off the floor of his car and licking them.

Oh, there we go, I thought, spotting a really big chunk of powder. Did I want to lick it? It didn't smell like anything. I was sure it was drugs, but... *I have to be sure. Lord, help me.*

I ate it and my mouth went numb.

I felt like an idiot sitting in the car outside for so long, especially since I was already late. But I put on a brave face and went inside.

One of the women I'd met at the conference opened the door and said, "Hi! I'm so glad you came. I didn't think you were going to make it."

I wanted to tell her everything right then and there. I needed to tell someone what was going on, but I was afraid of being ostracized. What was I supposed to say? *Hi, I'm Leah, and I have the taste of cocaine ransacking my taste buds. Please be my friend?*

It's challenging to ask for help when we have a loved one struggling with an addiction. There's the shame of not being "normal," of feeling like a burden from a life heavy-laden with drama. When my friends would ask me how I was, for once, I would have liked to sincerely say, "I'm great! Things are going well for me!" Instead I did all I could not to pull a face while deciding whether it was appropriate to tell of the most recent drama.

As much as I wanted to talk about my husband's addiction, talking to someone who didn't understand what I was going through was sometimes harder than keeping it to myself.

I'm sure if my friends and family had seen my life depicted on the big screen, they would have told me to leave Grander many times over. I would have told myself to go, had God ever set me free. Instead I did the best I could. I was content enough to create emotional and physical space, leave the situation when I thought it was causing harm, and encourage my husband to seek treatment. I even prepared separation papers with a lawyer, but I never served him.

I felt peace about the choices I'd made.

Some people who struggle with addiction abuse their loved one's compassion on a regular basis. They put their spouses "in their place" to make sure they know how unhappy they are having to meet such "unrealistic expectations." Like a slow-boiling pot of water, the spouse can unknowingly warm to their loved one's emotional twisting—abuse, apologize, manipulate, retreat—until they're surrounded by the inferno that was once their lives and cannot move on. Stuck and afraid, they think, *I should have left sooner. I should have seen it coming.*

Should have, could have, if only... but Jesus weeps for them. Jesus wants them to know He is the water (John 7:37–39), the fountain of life (Psalm 36:9). He won't let them be burned when they walk through the flames.

> When you pass through the waters, I will be with you, and the rivers will not overwhelm you. When you walk through the fire, you will not be scorched, and the flame will not burn you.
> —Isaiah 43:2

There's a lot of judgment for women who stay with an addicted or abusive spouse. "What's wrong with her?" people wonder. I say, let them talk. They'll forget about it in a week. Surround yourself with people who see your strength in staying. It's admirable to honour someone whom God has painfully called you to love.

There's a reason most colleges offer honorary degrees, overlooking accreditation in recognition of life experience. Many leaders learned more about their faith in the trenches of desperation than at Bible college.

In the same way, God has called, chosen, appointed, and placed honour upon those who have the call of evangelism on their lives. If you've been struggling to remain firm in your faith because everything continues to go wrong, see it as a promotion. Yes, things are bad, but God is preparing you to be a light in dark places.

You are in the process of becoming qualified.

> In every situation take up the shield of faith with which you can extinguish all the flaming arrows of the evil one.
> —Ephesians 6:16

I'm sure I was the only woman in the Bible study that day who had the taste of cocaine in her mouth, but I wasn't the only one with marital problems, or who had been devastated about a dream that had failed to come to fruition, or who had experienced deep grief or loss. A scar is a scar, no matter what caused the wound in the first place.

In a world that's becoming increasingly impersonal, it's more important than ever to share our pain. We should be brutally blunt and honest about what has hurt us, and tell of how very terrible we are and all the rotten things we've done. When we're all there together in that blunt and rotten place, we can empathetically say, "You know what? I've been in a similar dark place before. You've got a friend in me."

My blog grew to help women who suffer from the pain of a spouse's addiction. I passionately continued on because it helped my faith and convictions to grow stronger every day. I was driven to right the wrong mindset we have about addiction and those who struggle with it.

But deep down, I did it because I needed to know that there was someone out there who understood what it felt like to be me.

CHAPTER TWENTY-SIX

blue eyes

Once some time had passed since my husband's relapse, things began to recover at home. We planned a trip to Canada to visit my parents and attend the gala for the award my book had won. I looked forward to getting dressed up for a fancy evening out.

My parents came to the gala with my husband and me. We ate a lovely meal, I collected my award, and much to my surprise we found out my screenplay had also won in its category. We had our photos taken in front of a movie-star-style banner and I felt a sense of accomplishment like I'd never felt before.

I hadn't been back to the town I'd grown up in for almost a decade, because my parents had relocated, but I thought it would be fun to show my husband my humble beginnings. I took him to eat at a local cafe. The name and owner had changed, but it was in the same spot as always. And the food was excellent, by the way! New Jersey may have the seal of perfection for Italian food, but Canada knocks it out of the park for farm-to-table freshness. We took our lunch to go and sat on a bench overlooking the pier, lined with familiar boathouses. It was the same peaceful, beautifully chipped picture it had always been.

There was a new antique store in town my mother kept telling me to go see, so we headed there next. I spent hours in that store. Grander came and went as I window-shopped thousands of treasures from years gone by. An antique wicker flower basket caught my eye. I ogled old doors, imagining how beautiful they would look in my home if only I could figure out how to get the hundred-year-old glass safely back to New Jersey. I didn't think they would make it tied to the top of my husband's car, but I was more than eager to try. Doors like that only come along once in a lifetime, you know.

I wandered around, lost in thought as I tried to figure out how I was going to tie two particularly gorgeous doors to the top of our car. Then I saw a pair of familiar bright blue eyes smiling at me beneath long eyelashes.

I knew those eyes.

Panic shot through me and I was jolted out of my thoughts. For three seconds, I was sure I was about to die right there, making myself another relic of years gone by.

I quickly recovered from my blast from the past, realizing that the face I was looking at belonged to the Fish's father, not the Fish himself. Phew! Crisis averted.

Except it wasn't. To be totally honest, it set me back for a moment. The Fish's dad talked to my mom like an old pal. I stood there smiling and nodding along, but my thoughts raced. *Geez, you have the same eyes. Is that what he's going to look like when he's his father's age? He's aging pretty well, although he's shorter than I remember. Wait, am I wearing my tall shoes? I can't remember. Don't look down.*

When the man said something funny, I pretended to get the joke.

Oh my gosh, he's talking about his son now. Don't listen. Wander away. Oh, look! Vintage jewellery. That looks really nice. I wonder how much that necklace costs? Now he's talking about what a great father the Fish is. I always knew he would be. He was always good with kids.

Now I feel sad. That's stupid, I'm married!

I wonder if the Fish ever thinks about me? What if his family reads my book? What if they read my book and give it to him? Maybe I should get ahead of the nightmare and mail him the book. No, that would be stupid. Don't mail the book. He's never going to read it. Are you legally required to tell someone you wrote a book and they're in it? What if he wanted to meet for coffee to discuss the legalities of removing him from a book he never agreed to be in? I couldn't do that… my husband would be so angry. Besides, he probably doesn't even drink coffee. Ooh, look at those crystal doorknobs…

"How are you?" his dad asked me.

Crap.

"Oh, um, I'm good. I have more kids. Just here... shopping..." I have no idea what I bumbled.

My mom asked him if he would take us to the secret storeroom where they kept "all the good stuff," but by then I only wanted to escape.

Great! Now I'm going to be trapped in a basement with the blue eyes and all my memories. Where's my husband? Gone when I need him, as usual.

We were going to the storeroom. Down the stairs I went, feeling cautious. And sure enough, this was indeed where all the good stuff was. Oh, the doors. This had just gotten real.

Bedazzled by the jewels, I wandered around the storeroom and came upon another set of blue eyes. I didn't have a panic attack this time, but it was the Fish's mother. She and I were Facebook friends.

When I'd started my anonymous blog, I had accidentally invited everyone I personally knew to follow my Instagram account. I'd then proceeded to frantically block them all, except for the Fish's older sister. It hadn't felt right to block her.[26]

I had a nice chat with the Fish's mother. She was so sweet, and it occurred to me that she would have been a great mother-in-law. This only made me feel more flustered.

Grander finally came back. I introduced him and we left shortly after, leaving both doors—and my past—behind us.

What a day! I didn't tell my husband who he'd just met. What would have been the point? It shouldn't have mattered.

But it did.

---

26 #mostlikelytoreadthisbook

CHAPTER TWENTY-SEVEN

wildflower

When my life reached its pinnacle of difficulty, I retreated to fantasy. I imagined what could have been or what hadn't happened yet, as if I was living in a movie inside my head. If you've ever had a spouse struggle with addiction, you'll know what I mean when I say that my husband wasn't generally a part of that fantasy. It had nothing to do with love or a lack thereof. The perfect escape fantasy had to be a complete departure from my daily reality. I couldn't physically run away anymore, so I took up running in my head.

Things were very hard after I made that trip home to Canada. I'd been happier and more relaxed there. In fact, I had gone backward so much since moving back to New Jersey that I was angry at my husband just for having married me. I didn't wish to have married the Fish instead, but he was often the hero in my escape fantasies—he changes his life and we meet again post-divorce. In one dream, we even met in heaven!

I want to be as honest as I can, because after helping women with spouses fight addiction for so long, I know I'm not the only "mental runner." It is tremendously important to get a handle on this type of dangerous thinking before it becomes a part of our reality.

When life with my husband was peaceful, I didn't think this way. It was only when familiar troubles arose, and it was likely a psychological reaction to post-traumatic stress. Maybe escaping into a fantasy is a common coping method during a triggering episode. I wouldn't know, because our finances were a wreck and we still couldn't afford therapy.

The majority of the time, these dreams of mine weren't intentional; they came about when I was sleeping. I'd go to bed feeling anxious and have vivid dreams of my life changing. To psychoanalyze myself, I believe the reason I dreamed of the Fish is simple: he was the boy I loved during the easiest years of my life.

It's possible the Fish didn't give me another moment's thought after he ditched me on my nineteenth birthday, but I'd been to many a therapist, wise advisor, intercessor, pastor, and friend to discuss how to break my emotional ties with him. Nothing made it go away until I met Grander. Sadly, my husband's addiction shattered the foundation of our relationship. Yes, I loved him, but I no longer trusted him with my heart. I would have rather reserved my heart for a fantasy, one that could never hurt me because it wasn't real.

I know this happens in divorce, too. Emotional affairs, even when they're imaginary, are another way of breaking off a relationship. Trust is lost before love. What is a relationship without vulnerability? It's impossible to love someone you fear will hurt you.

We do the same thing with God. After patiently waiting for the blessings we're sure we've been promised for our suffering, we lose hope and stop being vulnerable because we no longer trust God with our heart's desire. If we don't trust Him, we cannot love Him.

It's not always right to pull away from pain and protect ourselves, but it's a natural human instinct. God understands. It's a guttural, animalistic response to keeping ourselves safe. An unspoken boundary of the soul. But pulling away can protect us as much as it can hurt us, and the key is learning to be wise in our pain.

The world tells us what safety looks like. It's a recently updated, well-decorated, air-conditioned house in a suburban neighbourhood. A new vehicle with fully loaded airbags, automatic brakes, and assisted parking. It's an award-winning school with a challenging curriculum that cultivates each individual child. We put prices on these worldly things. The safer something is, the more expensive it is. Try to find an affordable single-family home in a decent neighbourhood with parking and a great school district in Manhattan!

That's why we lived in New Jersey.

God's Word tells us not to worry about our safety. When Jesus spoke about God providing for the birds of the air, He was saying that our safety isn't found in material things but in God. The title of that lesson in the Christian Standard Bible is "The Cure for Anxiety" (Matthew 6:25–34). Sounds like something our world desperately needs, doesn't it?

Our personal, physical, and emotional security should be built on who we are to Christ. As Matthew 6:33 says, *"But seek first the kingdom of God and his righteousness, and all these things will be provided for you."*

We often hear the message to seek the Kingdom of God. I've wondered if we covet material things because they reflect what the world will be like when it's restored to God's people, with its streets of gold and precious gems. Perhaps we're trying to create our own version of heaven on earth.

I think it's also religious to despise beautiful things. We shouldn't let covetousness make us prideful, but the Bible says that we are co-heirs with Christ (Romans 8:17). It's not a fantasy to believe we are queens and princesses and should be treated as such here on earth.

We place less emphasis on the second half of Matthew 6:33: *"and all these things will be provided for you."* I'm not saying we should chase money or find security in possessions, but clothing, shelter, and the like will be given to us by God.

> *And why do you worry about clothes? Observe how the wildflowers of the field grow: They don't labor or spin thread. Yet I tell you that not even Solomon in all his splendor was adorned like one of these. If that's how God clothes the grass of the field, which is here today and thrown into the furnace tomorrow, won't he do much more for you—you of little faith?*
>
> —Matthew 6:28–30

If your spouse has drifted from God and the foundation of your relationship, and if your identity has been shaken, know that you are unequally yoked right now. I can't tell you what to do about your spouse because each situation is unique, but as for yourself, take time to seek first the Kingdom of God. Seek His truth about you. Ask God to show you the dreams He has for you. Pursue Him as your purpose and let that be your fantasy! Dream of God, wildflowers, and the splendour that awaits you in heaven.

Jesus is our bridegroom, but He won't leave us feeling unsatisfied. He will fulfill all our desires in His lovingkindness and sustenance. He's a most excellent husband and I pray that you desire to be His excellent wife. Don't let your mind stray from He who loves you most.

> Of this one thing I am certain: Jesus is the only man who can make our wildest dreams come true.

Of this one thing I am certain: Jesus is the only man who can make our wildest dreams come true.

CHAPTER TWENTY-EIGHT

oh, baby

You've got to be kidding me, I thought as I waited for the pregnancy test to stop lying to me.

"No. No way. There's no way," I said to no one in particular.

It's fine, I'll take another one.

It wasn't fine. The second test was a liar, too.

I sat on the toilet in my bathroom with its black and salmon art deco-style tiles, trying to wrap my head around the news. I went online and searched for "what causes a false pregnancy," holding out hope that perhaps my vitamins had caused the discrepancy.

It turns out that vitamins don't cause false pregnancies—which I knew, because this was baby number three. Three kids! I had just turned thirty! How could I have three kids already? Most of my friends didn't even have one!

At the time, I had just begun to look into college classes to return to school. I was speaking to the admissions teams about getting a business degree. Yes, business—the only class I'd failed in university. I was no longer comfortable relying on my husband for anything, let alone trusting that he would be financially responsible. It was time to make my own income and stop being dependent on my husband. I realized later that the timing of the baby was God's way of saying, for the second time, "You need to be dependent on Me."

Fear, anxiety, babies-crying-at-three-in-the-morning thoughts tornadoed around my head.

It's going to be okay, I tried to tell myself, but nothing felt okay. It felt like the minuscule piece of okay that I'd managed to get back was being stolen, chewed up, and spat out before being crushed by an egocentric luxury car.

I told my husband through tears that I was pregnant. He responded considerately by telling the world—first my family, then his, then Facebook. It was literally a matter of minutes before my grief had been shared all over the internet, before I'd had a chance to absorb it.

How dare he?! I angrily thought. *That's just like him, to share the news while I'm still crying. How insensitive can one person be?!*

My shock over the pregnancy turned into a blazing Irish rage with one target: my husband. Which of course only made matters worse, because I was now pregnant with his offspring and shouldn't be getting angry; it was bad for the baby.

I felt guilty for being upset about my pregnancy. It wasn't that I didn't love babies. I did. I love my babies more than anything in the world. And I wanted a girl, badly.

But I wasn't ready to have another child with Grander. I didn't think he had been able to stay sober long enough. He wasn't as honest as I wanted. And I always had a deep-seated, unsettled feeling that he'd been unfaithful at some point in our marriage. The pregnancy reminded me that things weren't "normal."

In that moment, my relationship felt like a devastating letdown.

Was this my fault? Where had I gone wrong in the becoming-a-grownup department? Not only had I gotten pregnant, pregnant, and pregnant again, but I wasn't emotionally stable enough to be a supermom and go back to school while getting ready for baby number three.

"You can still get a job," my well-meaning friends said.

"You can still go to school," my husband said.

Actually, no. I couldn't. Not with three kids, the husband I had, my high stress level and lack of support, my history of high-risk pregnancies, and seeing absolutely no light at the end of the tunnel.

No.

At one point in my life, I could have picked myself up from that. Like I had at the age of twenty-one when I'd became pregnant with my eldest son.

But now I was broken. The pregnancy brought with it a fight against situational depression and I had no energy left. I was finished. And I had a panic disorder to boot. The only thing I knew how to do was be a mom, take care of my kids, and look to Jesus for hope.

It's a good thing I didn't try to do it all, too, because the first trimester happened to be the roughest I'd ever had. I was sick all day long, every day. I threw my neck out and couldn't move my head. I got vertigo from the stress, and there were days when I was so dizzy I could hardly stand.

Grander and I fought until our marriage was the tensest it had been since he was in active addiction. Thankfully, it was still summer break, so I left with my boys and went home to Canada for a breather. I only intended to stay for a week or two but ended up staying for a month. It was the most relaxed I had been in a long time. I started to feel like myself again. Hope returned, and I felt motivated and encouraged.

Within a few days of returning home, I was back to feeling sick. My jaw locked from clenching back my angry, hormonal words, and I lost all my motivation to write and encourage the women following my blog. I did what I could to get through each day: to be a mom, to take care of my kids, and to look to Jesus for hope.

One day in particular, I started to feel better. My husband had told me he'd relapsed while the children and I were gone, so I decided to clean our home both physically and spiritually. As each room sparkled, I felt more at peace.

While cleaning my basement television room, listening to worship music, underneath the sofa I found a small empty bag that had undoubtedly held drugs.

My body went into shock as I tried to stop the lightning anger that flashed into existence. I tried not to call my husband and instead attempted to recapture the feelings of accomplishment I'd had only a few moments before.

It didn't work.

At precisely the wrong time, my husband sent me a text message and I returned it with a picture of the empty bag. He didn't respond, which only made me angrier.

I called him. At the time, I believed I was going to resolve the conflict calmly, but the truth is that the battle was only with myself. My husband was fine, wholly absorbed in his work and not giving much more than a thought to my anxieties. And isn't that the way it often is when we feel that someone has wronged us? We're wrapped up in the pain of it, still reliving the experience, while the other party has all but forgotten about the incident, if they even realize it's happened at all?

Pain is personal.

My day was lost. I succumbed to the whispers of the enemy, which told me that things would never change, that my children were going to be scarred for life, and that I had two choices: stay and be hurt, or leave and somehow raise the three of them on my own.

I went into my bedroom and sobbed as I had done only a handful of times before. I mourned my relationship. I wept for my unborn child's future. I had lost all hope.

This time, I was ready to give up on my husband—forever.

CHAPTER TWENTY-NINE

forgiveness

TIME AND AGAIN, I'VE SEEN PREGNANCY SPARK TROUBLE IN A SPOUSE recovering from addiction. What's supposed to be a happy time ends up being dangerously stressful.

We know stress isn't good for babies, but the babies of women like myself have undergone an immense amount of stress. I'm biased, but by the grace of God my babies all turned out wonderful.

Still, I'm not the only one whose husband seemed to lose his good sense during a pregnancy. Many women have come into my online support group saying, "Yay! I'm pregnant! It's a new start! God blessed us!" Within the first couple of months, they're back saying, "I have to leave! I can't do this anymore! I have to raise this child alone!" Difficulty does not remove the blessings of God.

> *Test me, Lord, and try me; examine my heart and mind. For your faithful love guides me, and I live by your truth.*
> —Psalm 26:2–3

Sure, it would be nice if life were simple and easy, but where in the Bible does it say that the easy life is a blessed life? *Au contraire, mon cher.* Jesus said that His yoke was easy (Matthew 11:30), but following Him would be the narrow way.

How many marriages do you know of firsthand where the couple has made it through addiction and come out the other side? It is a very, very narrow way.

I believed I would be blessed for loving my husband whether he cleaned up his act or not, but deep down I felt I would be more blessed if he sobered up. If my husband became a new man, surely it would be a sign that God loved me and saw my faithfulness.

It's wrong to follow God because of what He can do for us. God didn't want my obedience; He wanted my love. My husband's healing, or lack thereof, had nothing to do with my personal relationship with God. At the time, I wasn't thinking clearly because my heart was in a desperate place. I didn't want to be a believer who knew God could heal people and yet didn't expect it to happen. Why not my husband? My husband's life was just as valuable as anyone else's. His turnaround would be a gift to our children and myself, and a testimony to God as well. I had no good reason to believe God *wouldn't* heal him.

I understood it could take time for my husband to find absolute healing from his addiction, but I knew God was with me, and I knew which path I wanted to take: the narrow way.

Reminded of this decision, I settled in for the long haul. Even though I was thoroughly heartbroken, I kept my eyes focused on the view in front of me—not where we were currently, or what I could see, but where God would take us.

As my husband improved mentally and emotionally, I was shocked to find that the most difficult part of recovery is actually living recovered. To be pregnant and act normal. To ask my husband to watch the children for an hour so I could get a much-needed pedicure. To have a man in the home who helped with dinner and the children.

Grander didn't have much experience with children or domestics at that point, except for the months he'd worked in the treatment centre cooking with expired grocery store leftovers, making meals for lonely, hungry men. Soup. It hadn't been gourmet, but it was a hit.

He still thinks he's an excellent chef. He has many gifts and talents, but I doubt making soup is one of them. Nor is seasoning chicken.

As it was, I didn't know how to be normal anymore.

I started to experience new forms of anxiety over the expectation that I was supposed to adjust to my newly sober husband, whose recovery seemed to be sticking for the first time ever. He tried to get us to do things with other couples, but I made excuses.

One time, we were driving by a local park when some new friends from church invited us to meet them there for a picnic. We were right there. We had no other plans. And it was a lovely park, too—a miniature Central Park with a playground, archery area, dog park, tennis court, racetrack, baseball diamond, and football and soccer fields.

This park had been a huge selling point for us when we'd moved to New Jersey. I had dreamt of afternoons lounging lazily on the "authentic" Mexican blanket I'd ordered from eBay for $7 while the children played at the playground or kicked their ball in the field. In reality, when we visited I had to run around from one playground apparatus to the next, chasing my kids because it was too large and busy to properly watch a four-year-old in the suburb where we lived.

As I was saying, our new friends invited us to the park. Even though we were right there, I declined. In fact, I didn't even tell my husband about the invitation until it was too late to go. I don't remember what excuse I made, only the feeling of desperately not wanting to sit on my $7 blanket and watch a so-called normal couple be normal. It hurt too much.

It took a long time for those feelings to fade. I was angry and still didn't trust Grander. He claimed that my problem was the distrust, which made me even more mad. I was irritated that he'd had years of support while I'd had none, left to pick up the pieces from the destruction of his addiction. I was lonely and afraid of the future. I was a hot mess!

The hardest thing of all was realizing that what I really needed was the one thing I didn't want to give him: forgiveness.

Throughout my pregnancy, Grander was the healthiest he had ever been in our marriage. But it wasn't picture-perfect, and it was never easy. I had panic attacks often and thought I was going to lose the baby from stress.

I didn't feel safe with my husband, but I wanted our marriage to work out. Being pregnant brought out deep vulnerabilities I hadn't even known I had.

Looking back, I can see now how much we grew in that season. Not only did God work on our marriage and the wounds I needed healing from, but He finished teaching me how to fully rely on Him. His Word over my life was king and the loving, caring, nurturing relationship I had with Him, and which I relied upon for strength, was so good that it spilled over into my husband's life as well. By holding onto Jesus, I felt Him holding onto the both of us.

The power of relationship extends far beyond what our Sunday school teachers taught us about the love of God. We were created to be in relationship. We were created to love and be loved. It's the very essence of who we are and who God is. When we put love (God) in the centre of our pain, and make love (God) the basis of all our decisions and choices, establishing love (God) as our motivation, goal, mission, and heart's desire, we receive the blessing of being in a deep relationship with Him.

To be in a relationship like that, we have to be willing to be vulnerable. If there's one area where we fail as a human race, it's being vulnerable. We expose everything but who we really are.

The world will tell you to detach, disconnect, and run away from your addicted loved one, but I say be brave enough to be vulnerable. Have boundaries, but share your heart. Be wise, but love the person beyond their addiction and expect good things to come. Pray for healing and hope for the miracle.

Most of all, forgive them, because they know not what they do.

Blessed [inwardly peaceful, spiritually secure, worthy of respect] are the gentle [the kind-hearted, the sweet-spirited, the self-controlled], for they will inherit the earth.

—Matthew 5:5, AMP

Worst case scenario, you'll have the peace of knowing that you behaved in a way you can be proud of. Best case, God will move in your life and change your situation for the better.

CHAPTER THIRTY

brenda

Time went on, and for the first time ever I had the chance to be happy about one of my pregnancies. I had recently found out that the baby I was carrying was a little girl, at long last! I couldn't wait to decorate a girl's nursery and have a baby shower bursting with pink gifts and hairbows. There I was with the perfect baby bump, gloriously shiny hair, and glowing pregnancy skin.

But where was my husband?

Unfortunately, in his sobriety, Grander had taken up a second life as a teenager. His new job was in a young, hip environment and he soaked it up like a sponge. Mind you, when I visited I didn't see too many young, hip people; I saw more young, tech-oriented people. That was fitting, since I thought Grander was wearing an alternate persona in order to fit in there. He grew his hair long, which never looks good on him no matter how many times he tries it. He also started wearing jeans and casual T-shirts to work. He listened to way more rock music and bought himself a longboard. Then, an electric skateboard. He told me it was a gift, but I don't believe that's true.

You must understand that living with someone on a recovery journey isn't easy. I would dare to say it's harder than the active addiction itself. When someone is addicted, you know what to expect: the money will be gone, they cannot come home high, everything is a lie, end of chapter. In recovery, though, the money is still gone, but they're not necessarily on drugs. They often replace their addiction with something else, or they get very depressed, to the point that everything feels like a lie. In active addiction, the lines are more obviously drawn. In recovery, you're in a grey area.

While I was with child, my husband became a child. Awesomesauce.

Still new to the area, I went back to thinking about making friends and building a support system. As though by heavenly timing, our church hosted a lunch for expectant mothers. I put on my most fabulous Carrie Bradshaw shoes, which I never did anymore, and drove to the estate of the host, located on a street lined with mansions. Estate is the correct word; it was quite impressive.

When I arrived, there were probably ten to fifteen other women there, each at different points in their pregnancies. They had dainty snacks, which I was a bit disappointed about because I was starving, but I put on my best social smile and tried to mingle.

A vivacious woman named Brenda taught and encouraged us. She was funny, beautiful, well-educated; I felt instantly inadequate. You see, Brenda got pregnant while studying to become a lawyer. Her pregnancy woes had been along the lines of "Do I have to give up on school?" Later, after she'd committed to seeing it through, her question was "Can I balance a baby and this career?" She could. She did. She had a very supportive husband and had hired a nanny.

Let me pause there.

Women like Brenda, God bless her, are the bane of my existence. Educated, financially sound, had a baby later in life, had a super supportive husband and a nanny… I can hardly bear it.

The entire time she was talking, I tried to not cry—hormonally, hangrily—since I was sitting in the seat right next to her. Her talk hit every single one of my biggest pain points: she was a successful lawyer with a happy marriage and four kids and her nanny rocked. As the women began to share, I realized there were more of them. Without exaggeration, all the women who shared had lucrative careers, supportive husbands, and childcare.

To be fair, not all the women shared.

I didn't go back to school when I found out I was pregnant. Why? Because I couldn't handle the workload, my other children, and my husband along with it. My sober husband had abandoned me in his midlife crisis, and in that moment, when I had vulnerably gone out to make friends, I found myself unbearably alone, in a room full of pregnant Brendas.

I tried to shake myself out of my self-pity to listen as the women shared their baby concerns with the group. I was one of the few who had multiple children.

Okay, it's fine, I thought. *I can share mama wisdom. I'm still a great mom! Breathe!*

I've forgotten all the concerns those women shared, except one. This woman and her husband were best friends and always got along. But oh boy, they had one area that had recently become difficult and they couldn't get past it. It was becoming a *real* problem.

I was so ready for the real talk to start.

The woman explained that they were fighting all the time because… she didn't want their future children to sleep in their bed and her husband thought they should be allowed to during thunderstorms and the occasional cuddle. They could not agree. She felt it would ruin the child.

It was a real problem—

"Are you serious?" I interrupted. "Stop worrying about something that hasn't even happened yet!"

I don't know if what I had to say made any sense, but essentially I said that the baby was still in her belly and they were having a fight over the child sleeping in their bed. I was thinking, *This is ridiculous!*

I should have stopped there, but instead I went on.

"Figure it out after the baby comes into the world. Some people have *real* problems," I said as tears began to form. "And their kids turn out all right. My husband had a drug addiction, a *drug* addiction, and my kids are fine. Your kid will be beautiful. You are going to spend many years worrying about your kid and it's a waste to spend a perfectly good pregnancy worrying about *that!*"

I stopped talking—and waited. Surely someone else at the table would have bigger problems than this. Was this what normal couples fought about?!

Nothing. No one.

Brenda looked at me with an expression that might have been pity or surprise. I can't say.

I left feeling more discouraged than ever. I drove home in a daze, parked the car, called my mom, and sobbed into the steering wheel.

CHAPTER THIRTY-ONE

flora

THE BIGGEST BENEFIT OF NOT HAVING FRIENDS OR A HUSBAND around is that God really becomes your everything. As my pregnancy went on and I grew in intimacy with God, I felt better and better about my husband and his recovery. Our life together wasn't perfect, but it was progress.

We spent the night of my labour waiting in the hospital, excited for our future. I knew I was jinxing it, but I said, "I can't believe our lives are so happy and normal right now!"

As if to say "This isn't over yet," our baby girl's heartbeat stopped twice during delivery before she finally arrived in the middle of the night. We named her Flora Grace. Flora, after my great-grandmother Alice Flora, and Grace, because without it she wouldn't have existed.

My husband went into work early the next morning for a meeting. He was sure it was about a promotion, but much to his surprise the company let him go. Yes, he was let go from the dream job we had returned to New York for.

Lord, really? That had to happen right now?!

You see, for years I had been praying that Grander would get fired. I was sure it was the only way he would take seriously his need for personal change. Year after year, people had failed to spot his high-functioning addiction, and he'd gotten away with it. Every. Single. Time. Drug testing? No problem. The company he used to work for would give their employees plenty of warning. And even when his addiction did show itself, his former boss was unbelievably understanding.

This new employer had been stringent. I hoped they would catch him in the act, but I didn't pray for it to happen post-conception! The timing was unbelievable.

Even more unbelievable, they hadn't fired him for doing drugs, since he was sober at the time. They fired him for breaking one of their many stringent rules.

Spirit of pride removed, my husband finally cut his hair. Praise, Jesus!

His employer graciously offered to extend our health insurance until the end of the month. Honestly, America, get it together. I won't go off on a rant about the healthcare system, but I think it's a catastrophic human rights violation.

I felt protected by God at that moment. I knew to the core of my being that God had extended the healthcare for my sake. He wanted me to know that I would be taken care of.

I won't go into the details of why my husband was let go, but to make a long story short it was a long time coming, a hard lesson in humility. He took out most of his pain on my mother, who stayed with our other children while I recovered in the hospital, instead of me. I tried to be emotionally strong and courageous, but I was terrified.

Would this set him off on another drug binge?

Would he be able to get another job?

Would he try to take his own life?

Would we have to move and leave the beautiful nursery I had worked so hard on?

I wanted the birth of this child to be a new start. I was ready for a new chapter, and a new and improved husband.

Grander, who had left that morning feeling overjoyed and hopeful for his future, returned red-eyed and defeated. I gave him a hug and my usual chipper banter. He was surprised that I was in such high spirits, which was due to ebbing back and forth between shock and the peace of the Holy Spirit.

He reached out to hold our one-month-premature baby girl, five pounds and fourteen ounces, and his eyes flooded with tears. She looked up at him in wonder. Grander put his index finger beneath her delicate little hands and buried his face into her blanket.

It was the saddest thing I've ever seen him do.

A few moments later, my mother came in with the boys and forced my husband to pull himself together. But I'm sure he sobbed himself to sleep that night.

For the next few weeks, Grander was in a worrisome state of mind. There was a period of time when he was able to be home and help me with the baby and children, but he was operating on autopilot. He wasn't enjoying his precious time with the kiddos or the fact that he was able to be home with me when I needed him. He couldn't find enjoyment in the baby, because every time he looked at her he felt like a failure.

Now, I realize that I'm speaking for him, but it's crucial to the story.

After a couple weeks of feeling like a loser, my husband turned to the one thing he thought would always make him feel good. He relapsed. I had a new baby, an emotionally deteriorating husband, not enough money to pay the bills, health insurance about to end, and a budding ministry to run.

"Rest," God said. "Let him figure it out."

It was difficult to allow my husband to fall to his demise without interfering in it. In the past, I had felt it was right to help him, but now I needed to get out of God's way and trust Him. I wouldn't let this shake my faith. God was for me, not against me! (Romans 8:31)

My husband is a hard worker. Despite my feelings of mistrust and doubt, he has always made sure there was a roof over our heads and food on the table, two things for which I'm very grateful. Within twenty-four hours of losing his job, he secured another one. He had to take a $50,000–$60,000 annual pay cut, but we knew it wouldn't last forever. It was a short-term struggle, and God was rooting for us.

As much as my faith comforted me, Grander's new job didn't cover our bills. Our property insurance was more than our mortgage. When I'd dreamt of buying a home and took the time to crunch numbers and organize our finances, I hadn't planned on spending more on property insurance than on a mortgage.

For the record, we didn't have a huge property. Welcome to the greater New York City metropolitan area!

When I was a single mother, I'd always had just enough to get by. Even though my starting wage had been only $11 per hour and my rent

$850 plus utilities, God had provided for me out of the blue, giving me exactly what I needed through other people.

> *He will tend his flock like a shepherd; he will gather the lambs in his arms; he will carry them in his bosom, and gently lead those that are with young.*
>
> —Isaiah 40:11, ESV

Going into this season with my husband, I expected the same thing to happen.

It didn't.

Nothing was enough. There was no way to pay the bills and more kept coming in. Because my husband had relapsed, I insisted that he see a doctor to deal with his emotions and the loss of his job, but because of our lapse in insurance it ended up being significantly more costly than we'd expected.

Our debt climbed. It was one thing after another. My oldest son got a concussion and suffered mild whiplash while snowboarding and needed to see a chiropractor. The baby needed diapers and pacifiers. Baseball season was starting and came with expenses. Though we were being as thrifty as we could, we had to ask ourselves, which utility bill will get paid on which paycheck? Meanwhile, our medical bills from the baby's birth were held delinquent in a separate file.

I spent the majority of my free time post-postpartum working on my blog, but with the birth of the baby I couldn't put much time into it. The blog was costing me more to maintain than I made from it.

One month passed, then two months, and there still wasn't enough income to cover our growing costs.

The silver lining was that my husband maintained his sobriety following his relapse after losing his job, and things began to feel somewhat normal. While financial difficulties might have been enough to break up the average couple, it brought the two of us together. It was nice to bicker about something that wasn't related to drugs or mental health.

In case you're in this situation and don't have the same experience, it took time to get to this point—time for my husband to let me take over the family's finances. It nearly killed him to do it because he didn't trust me.[27] While finances can come and go, I didn't think we could rebuild a healthy marriage after losing it.

The relationship survival skills we'd practiced during addiction now came in handy in the "normal" world.

Although God didn't financially provide or make our bills go away, He did provide something much better: a marriage in repair.

We said we were broke but happy, this time both on the same page. I couldn't have wanted anything more.

---

27 I hadn't given much thought to him not trusting me before our financial struggles. He had been going through a lot while I was having vicious panic attacks. I was also jealous and angry... I was a whole lot of things. And I realized I wasn't behaving trustworthy for him either.

CHAPTER THIRTY-TWO

perfection

We have more in common than we realize. Sit in an airport for a few days and watch the people go by. They may have different hair, skin, and clothing, but ultimately they're all the same. We breathe the same after climbing twenty flights of stairs, we eat Sloppy Joes and spaghetti the same, our feet stink the same on a sweaty summer day. You're welcome for that picture! We have babies in the same painful way.

We paint ourselves in a rainbow of colours, but nothing totally erases the fact that, at our core, we are all alike.

We don't want to be the same; we want to be unique. But we don't realize that what makes us alike is the most special characteristic of all.

Did you know that every single person has a unique fingerprint, vein pattern, and retina? God gifted us our own identities. We have our own talents, our own thoughts. Yet we yearn for connection. We want to know there's someone out there who gets us, but we still leave our unique fingerprint on the world.

It's in finding this balance—of connecting where we're similar and celebrating how we're unique—that makes the world so beautiful. If we could only recognize that our similarities are more important than culture, skin colour, sexual preference, and religious background, we would find that connection we're all yearning for: love.

The older I get, the more I blossom into the person I was created to be. I'm much more serious than I thought I was. It's seriousness masked with humour and positivity. I take solace in the fact that I'm maturing. I may not do everything right, but I'm learning.

Wisdom is one quality I've always admired. You may have heard of Solomon in the Bible, but in case you haven't, he was a very wise king. Solomon had the opportunity to go down in history as one of the fairest and wisest men of all time, but he failed to do so because of his lust for women and money, which led him away from worshipping God. Solomon was one of the most materialistic men in the Bible, acquiring much and taxing the people so he could continue to consume more.

Much like an addiction, he chased something other than God to make himself feel good. God was angry at Solomon for his foolishness, yet moved by his desire for wisdom. Solomon's life stands as a lesson for us to be responsible with what God puts in our hands. It is also proof that we can be a sinner and a saint at the same time.

Our society today is consumed with lust and passions that lead people away from God. We face our surface issues without addressing our spirit of idolatry. Some people's problems are more visible than others, but in some ways I feel like that can be freeing because those people wear no masks of perfection.

Imagine if everyone in your life knew all your mistakes, and you also knew theirs?

Pause. Stop reading and think about this for a good sixty seconds. What if everyone knew about that time when you did _____, or when you said _____.

For many people, perfection has become the only acceptable image.

Being in the beauty industry, I was focused on looks for a long time. Granted, I cared about looks long before I became a hairstylist. When I was young, two haircuts were all the rage: the Jennifer Aniston (long, sleek, stick-straight, jagged front) and the Meg Ryan (short, wispy, bleach blond, perfect fluff). I wasn't a Jennifer Aniston or a Meg Ryan. I was more like a 1990s Debra Messing.

Unfortunately, I was born in 1986, which meant I was an adorable child in terrible clothing, and by the time the mid-90s hit, I was an awkward, knobby-kneed girl with freckles, no eyebrows, and a huge pouf of curly red hair. It wasn't the nice kind of curly; it was coarse with tiny bits of ginger fuzz popping up everywhere. It refused to curl nicely au natural, no matter how much of my dad's hair gel I put in.

When I was in Grade Two, I won a hair crimper for answering a math question right. I'd known one of the prizes was a peachy pink crimper, so this was the only time I ever worked so hard at math. And that crimped hair? Wow. That was before the era of the flatiron. How did I survive?! And no, you can't see a picture. Thankfully, I grew up in the era right before we started taking pictures of everything and posting them online to live on forever in a crimped eternity.

When I was older, I tried ironing out my hair to get rid of the fluff—with a real iron! I laid a towel on my bedroom floor, carefully fanned out my hair, and ironed it. I'd seen Barbara Streisand do this in *The Way We Were* and figured she was clearly a genius. This dangerous technique worked to achieve the perfect ponytail. It was ironed perfection for a fuzzy-headed ginger in a sleek, bleached 1990s world.

When I look back at my pictures now and see my Grade Seven self in my headband and JNCO acid-washed jeans I thought were so cool, I realize how utterly ridiculous I looked. I don't say that from a place of insecurity; I say it because it's painfully true.

This is just a funny example of normal growing-up behaviour, but what if we apply the same logic to our relationships? To our jobs? To our parenting? How many things will we look back on and say, "I was being ridiculous!"?

God clearly made men and women opposites to ensure we would need Him to make sense of one another. As 1 Corinthians 13:4 tells us, "*Love is patient, love is kind*" (NIV). That level of perfection in marriage will never be reached. So long as this is clearly communicated and understood beforehand, that's all right. Our imperfections are not problems. However, despite warnings from seasoned couples that love is a choice, and despite the number of people we see getting divorced, we live in a world that strives for perfection. Perfect, sleek, straight, wispy, bleach-blond perfection.

The human race, on the whole, is neither sleek nor perfectly unkempt. We are wild, crazy, untameable, unmanageable, frizzy, crazy, unpredictable, and all over the place. No amount of ironing will smooth us, or our relationships, enough.

The good news is that God is the answer. He likes fluffy and He made frizzy. Our circumstances are only bad if we see them that way.

Woah, wait. What?

Let me say that again: our circumstances are only bad if we see them that way!

See, I am doing a new thing! Now it springs up; do you not perceive it? I am making a way in the wilderness and streams in the wasteland.

—Isaiah 43:19, NIV

I spent many days trying to convince myself, "I believe God will heal my husband." I believed God could do it, but didn't believe He would.

After that statement became stale, I started saying, "I don't believe in my husband's ability to get better, but I believe in God's ability to heal him." On the surface, it sounds like a holy enough thing to say, but I was wrong to think so poorly of my husband. My husband is a son of God, perfectly made.

Jesus said He had to leave but would send the Holy Spirit to us, and we would do even greater works than He (John 6:7, 14:12), which means I should have believed in my husband's birthright and acknowledged his identity in Christ. I didn't give my husband's efforts credit for one victory. Not a one. I gave God all the praise.

Again, that seems perfectly religious, but my husband did his share. It's not easy to get into recovery and stay there, but he kicked the enemy's butt. I'm sure it helped to have a praying wife behind him, but my husband was the one who did the work. He chose to let God lead him, he chose to walk away from addiction, and he chose to support his family. He's the only one who could have made that choice. That's the honest truth.

Blessed is the man who remains steadfast under trial, for when he has stood the test he will receive the crown of life, which God has promised to those who love him.

—James 1:12, ESV

When it comes to leaving our unique fingerprint on the world, we have to be willing to do the difficult work, not the work that feels good. If we aren't willing to take risks and be vulnerable, God can't bless us.

I heard a sermon a long time ago that rocked my world. Apologetically, I can't remember who said it, but it went something like this: "Have you ever considered that God gave you this heavy mantle to carry not because you did something wrong, but because you did everything right?" That would mean that the reason you're here right now, loving the person you love, is that God knew you were the one who would be faithful enough, maybe even crazy and unkempt enough, to walk out the challenges you're in the middle of.

I would rather be a sinner who tried and failed than a saint who was indifferent.

> *So, because you are lukewarm, and neither hot nor cold, I am going to vomit you out of my mouth.*
> —Revelation 3:16

I was going to leave it at that, but I won't.

Like the Grinch, my heart has grown three times since the beginning of this story. I understand addiction in a way I would have never expected. I know who I am, what I'm supposed to be doing, and who God created me to be without being one hundred percent sure of myself or comfortable in my own skin. It took choosing to love someone through God's eyes for me to realize how deeply God loved me, too. He waits for us, fights for us, chases us, dreams of us, and yearns for us—and if it takes this ugly darkness to realize it… well, so be it. God has used my husband's addiction to change the darkness that lingered inside of me.

New York was the devil's apple for me, an idol that broke my heart, making the pain over my husband's addiction much worse. We all have these apples in our lives, a certain something Satan offers to give us the life we always dreamed of. He did it to Jesus in the desert before He set off to Galilee (Luke 4:1–14), just as he did to Eve in the Garden of Eden (Genesis 3:1–6), just as he did to me.

New York was my great temptation, but it wasn't the real issue; it was who I thought New York could make me. It became a part of my identity.

My affinity for the Big Apple changed the storyline of my family forever. It affected us all, from my Brady Bunch parents to my chicken-legged children. Thankfully, Jesus closes the gap between our sins and God. This is God's love story, after all. He is waiting for us to choose Him.

If we're very lucky, the smell of grace will permeate our sofa cushions, too.

CHAPTER THIRTY-THREE

skating

On a warm November day, my husband and I took the children to Bryant Park to go ice-skating. We took turns holding Flora, who was nine months old, and helping our four-year-old Denley learn how to skate while Beckett, who was much older now, glided in circles around us. After, we strolled through the Christmas Village and window-shopped some artisan goods.

My heart was happy. The sun was shining. There was no winter wind blowing through our jackets.

We stopped for a homemade donut, and later, a freshly made hot cocoa. It had a giant homemade marshmallow in the middle that melted into the dark chocolate as we sipped it. It tasted rich.

When we were full and happy, we packed up our things and walked through the city back to our car, drove home, and made a simple dinner.

It was a perfect day.

When I dreamed of moving to New York as a young woman—well, I'm still a young woman!—I dreamed that I'd write and spend my money on fabulous shoes. Big hair. Big dreams. Small apartment. While my dreams didn't come to fruition the way I had hoped, à la *The Devil Wears*

Prada,[28] God wrote me my own New York love story. It was a bit *Coyote Ugly*,[29] peppered with some *Save the Last Dance*,[30] and a dash of *Serendipity*.[31]

My love story looked like ice-skating in the park, smiling and laughing as I looked over to see my husband capturing the moment our son learned to skate. It looked like holding the hand of my handsome, curly-headed husband and following our children while they danced through the streets of New York, pushing a stroller with a baby girl nestled in grace. It looked like going home and making dinner as my husband sat on the sofa and checked his work email while the children ran around the house like chicken-legged hurricanes because they drank too much hot cocoa.

It looked like being exactly where I was. It was where I belonged.

If we can take ourselves out of our anxieties and restlessness to appreciate what we have around us, we may come to realize that life itself can be a dream. It's not comfortable or perfect, but it is a gift.

For those of us who have loved ones who've struggled with addiction, or are currently struggling, these joyful, peaceful moments may be few and far between, but that's precisely why we must grab hold of them so tightly.

There may come a day when you look back on photos of a happy time and realize, *He was high in those pictures*. Don't let it steal the happiness from the day you had together. Don't let Satan assault both your present and your memories of the past. Don't let him take your hope away. Don't let him ruin your children's futures. Don't let him come into your home to mess with your peace, and your marriage, and your career, and your laundry, and ruin your life. In the name of Jesus, no! Just no.

Don't let addiction stop you from dreaming. Believe. Raise your shield of faith (Ephesians 6:16). If the first dream didn't work out, God

---

28 A movie about a journalist who gets a job working for New York's biggest fashion magazine editor.
29 A movie about an aspiring singer from the country who finds herself singing in a sexualized manner in a bar in New York.
30 A movie about a Caucasian girl who finds herself confronting class and racial differences while pursuing her dream of dance.
31 A movie about a British girl and a New Yorker who let fate decide if they're meant to be together.

gives you freedom to dream again. Be bold in your trust of what you ask your Father for.

> *If you remain in me and my words remain in you, ask whatever you want and it will be done for you. My Father is glorified by this: that you produce much fruit and prove to be my disciples.*
> —John 15:7–8

Healing from addiction isn't too big for God. Total healing. Real recovery. The most important step is Jesus. If your spouse doesn't find recovery from their addiction and you don't find restoration for your marriage, I hope that today, right now, will mark the beginning of the recovery of your heart.

But a hot cocoa in the park doesn't hurt.

about the author

Leah Grey didn't want to become an addiction guru; hair-guru was more like it. Did you want to know what kind of haircut would flatter your face shape the best? She was your girl. Did you need to know what to do at 3 a.m. when your husband hadn't answered the phone and took $300 out of your joint bank account? No, thank you.

God often calls the most unqualified, resistant, and ill-spoken to do His Kingdom work. In a similar fashion, Leah is a wildly unqualified, three-time college dropout, whose husband says she can be mildly offensive at times. She has three hurricanes for children and little free time on her hands. She quit working as a hairstylist to write about what God did for her through her husband's addiction. Not because her life was perfect, but because she found unshakable peace in her daily chaos.

Leah is an award-winning writer whose online courses on boundaries and addiction blogs have reached over 350,000 women since it started in 2014. She created an online support group, Habit, that focuses on Biblical principles and advice for wives and partners of addiction. *No One Brings You a Casserole When Your Husband Goes to Rehab* is her debut book.

If you're tired and overwhelmed, and in need of a friend who gets it, visit Leah's website to contact her or access her free resource library:

leahgrey.com

CPSIA information can be obtained
at www.ICGtesting.com
Printed in the USA
BVHW042148090223
658258BV00004B/203